HISTORY EXPOSED

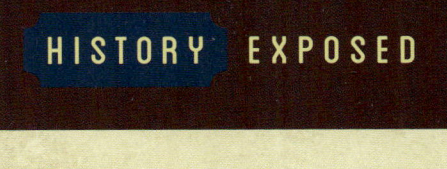

The Untold History of Henry VIII and the Tudors

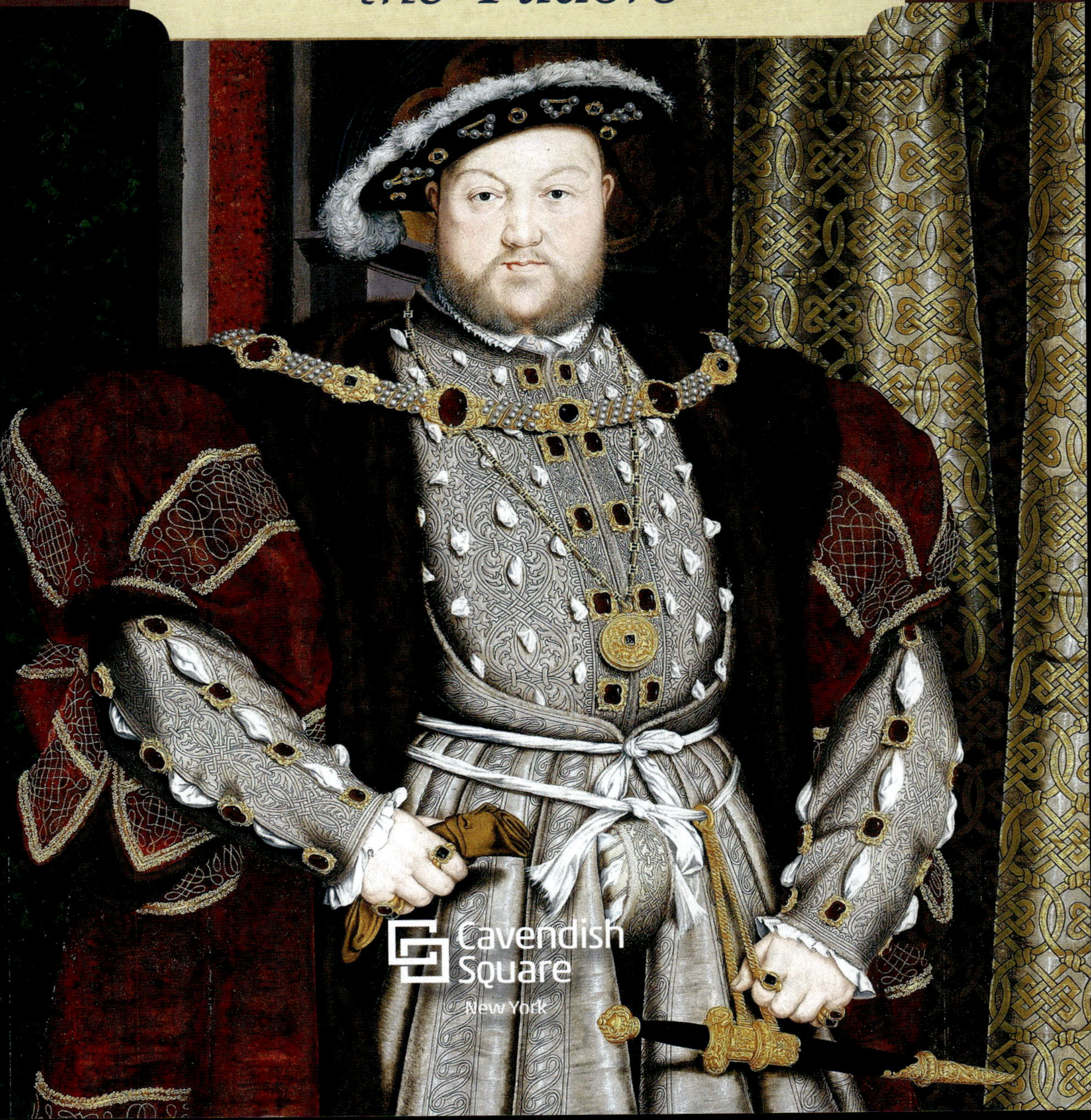

Cavendish Square
New York

The Untold History of Henry VIII and the Tudors

Published in 2017 by Cavendish Square Publishing, LLC
243 5th Avenue, Suite 136, New York, NY 10016

Copyright © 2017 Amber Books Ltd

First Edition

Cataloging-in-Publication Data

Names: John, Judith.
Title: The untold history of Henry VIII and the Tudors / Judith John.
Description: New York : Cavendish Square Publishing, 2017. | Series: History exposed | Includes index.
Identifiers: ISBN 9781502619044 (library bound) | ISBN 9781502619051 (ebook)
Subjects: LCSH: Henry—VIII—King of England—1491-1547—Juvenile literature. | Great Britain—History—
Henry VIII, 1509–1547—Juvenile literature. | Great Britain—History—Tudors, 1485–1603—Juvenile literature.
Classification: LCC DA332.J64 2017 | DDC 942.05'2'092—dc23

Editorial Director: David McNamara
Editor: Caitlyn Christensen
Art Director: Jeffrey Talbot
Designer: Amy Greenan
Production Assistant: Karol Szymczuk
Production Editor: Renni Johnson
Photo Research: J8 Media

The photographs in this book are used by permission and through the courtesy of: Wokshop of Hans
Holbein the Younger 1497/8/File:Workshop of Hans Holbein the Younger - Portrait of Henry VII -
Google Art Project.jpg/Wikimedia Commons, cover, 1; Hemis/Rieger Bertrand/Alamy, 2–3.

Printed in the United States of America

Metric Conversion Chart		
1 inch = 2.54 centimeters	1 mile = 1.609 kilometers	1 ton = 0.907 metric tons
1 foot = 30.48 centimeters	1 square foot = 0.093 square meters	1 pound = 454 grams
1 yard = 0.914 meters	1 square mile = 2.59 square kilometers	

CONTENTS

INTRODUCTION

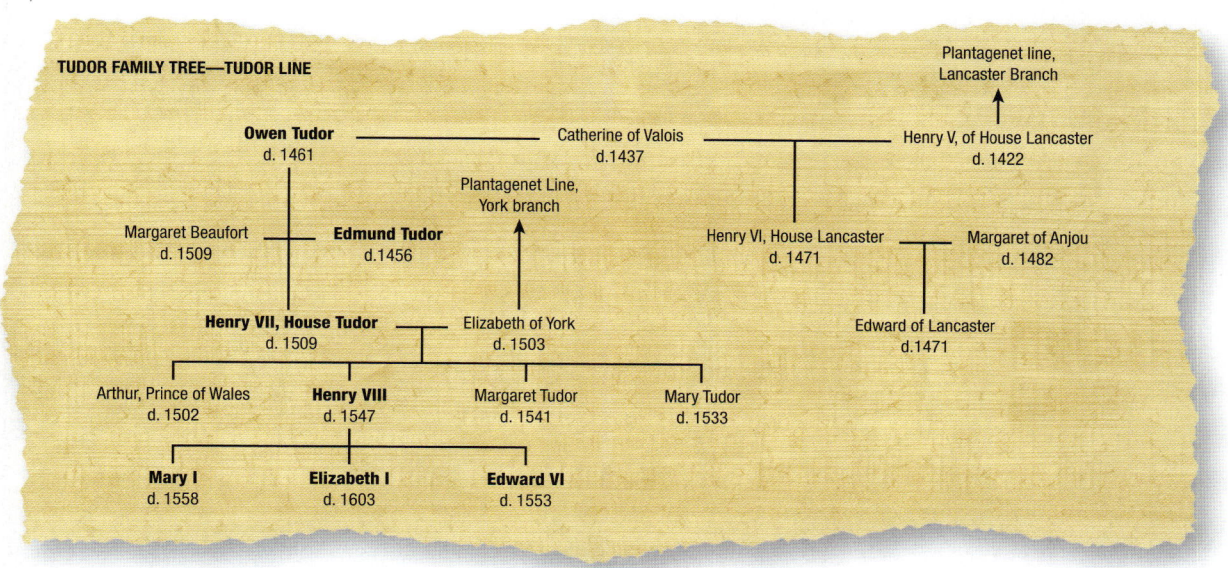

TUDOR FAMILY TREE—TUDOR LINE

Plantagenet line,
Lancaster Branch

Owen Tudor
d. 1461

Catherine of Valois
d.1437

Henry V, of House Lancaster
d. 1422

Plantagenet Line,
York branch

Margaret Beaufort
d. 1509

Edmund Tudor
d.1456

Henry VI, House Lancaster
d. 1471

Margaret of Anjou
d. 1482

Henry VII, House Tudor
d. 1509

Elizabeth of York
d. 1503

Edward of Lancaster
d.1471

Arthur, Prince of Wales
d. 1502

Henry VIII
d. 1547

Margaret Tudor
d. 1541

Mary Tudor
d. 1533

Mary I
d. 1558

Elizabeth I
d. 1603

Edward VI
d. 1553

Stretching back to the Middle Ages, the fortunes of the English monarchy have been wracked with violence, dishonor and bloodshed for centuries. A bloody trail of treason casts its dark shadow over England's mighty rulers, whose tales of treachery and personal intrigues have delighted, appalled and captivated for centuries.

Murder. Usurpation. Adultery. War. Long Live the Kings of England!

Edward III was King of England from 1327 to 1377. His heroic reign is known for sowing the seeds for government and an effective military force, achievements all the more laudable as they

Opposite: King Henry VI with his Queen Consort Margaret of Anjou. Margaret may look angelic, but she was a force to be reckoned with. She even ruled England when Henry VI was incapacitated.

followed the disastrous reign of his father, Edward II. Edward III sired 12 children. Two of his sons were made dukes—John of Gaunt was the first Duke of Lancaster and Edmund of Langley was the first Duke of York. Their descendants would plunge England into a civil war that would last for 30 years, only ending with peace when the Tudors took power in 1485, uniting the warring houses.

Getting to Know the Family

In an age where murder and duplicity came hand in hand with power and prestige, the origins of the Tudor

Above: This painting by Henry Payne, "Choosing the White and Red Roses" (1908) depicts the scene from Shakespeare's *Henry VI, Part I*, in which the warring houses of Lancaster and York and their supporters indicate their alliance by choosing red or white roses.

> Catherine … sought comfort in the arms of Owen Tudor … the humble wardrobe keeper of Catherine of Valois.

dynasty were formed. But before the Tudors came to rule, a series of murders, depositions, madness and imprisonment unfolded over the course of generations until the Tudors would bring an uneasy peace to the troubled shores of England.

John of Gaunt's grandson was the famously heroic King Henry V. It was Henry's actions during the Battle of Agincourt that won him France and the hand of Catherine of Valois, who became his wife in 1420. They had a son, but their joy was short-lived and Henry V died in 1422. Catherine, alone in a strange country, sought comfort in the arms of Owen Tudor (Owain Tewder in his native Welsh). Owen Tudor was the

humble wardrobe keeper of Catherine of Valois, the widowed wife of Henry V of the house of Lancaster. His lowly position meant the marriage was kept a secret at first, so no definite proof exists of the union.

Henry VI would inherit the English and French thrones from his father, but his youth and precarious mental state would be the cause of disputes, intrigues and violence. In 1445, Henry VI married the tempestuous Margaret of Anjou in an effort to restore peaceful relationships with France. Henry VI was

THE MIRACULOUS KING

SHORTLY AFTER HENRY VI's death, rumors abounded that he possessed saintly powers and could make miracles happen. "Bending a coin to King Henry" could reportedly cause miracles to happen, including providing healing powers and even preventing death. People would make the pilgrimage to his shrine. He was even close to being canonized during Henry VIII's reign.

Left: This painting shows Edward of Westminster as Edward IV's captive at Tewkesbury in 1471. It is believed that Prince Edward was dispatched by Edward IV's triumphant supporters.

Richard of York had a taste for power. Richard was supported by Richard Neville, known as Warwick the Kingmaker.

Ironically, Richard of York would never wear the crown himself, but two of his sons would, showing that they were just as capable of treachery as their wicked father. Richard of York and Neville raised an army against Henry VI, claiming the first victory on the field of Saint Albans in May 1455. The Yorkist victors then imprisoned the confused King in the Tower of London until Henry regained his senses in 1456, once again returning to his throne. Richard of York had shown his true colors. He fled to Ireland, returning in 1459, determined that this time Henry would not be so lucky. Henry was sent back to the Tower and Richard ruled as Protector of the Realm. While he was not King, this was almost as good.

Meanwhile, Margaret of Anjou had been tirelessly raising an army by building up Lancastrian support and forming an alliance with James III of Scotland. The warring houses clashed in an almighty battle at Wakefield and won a great victory of the house of Lancaster, in which Richard of York was killed.

pious and loving, but also weak and prone to mental breakdowns, a complete contrast to his forceful wife. Their son, Edward of Westminster, would die in battle in 1471, leaving the heir to the throne in doubt.

Taking advantage of Henry VI's instability, Richard, the third Duke of York, and Edmund, the Duke of York's grandson, were both appointed Lord Protector of England in 1454 when Henry VI had a nervous breakdown. By January 1455, Henry had recovered enough to take back control of his country, but by then

Henry's descent into madness continued until Richard's son, Edward of York, took over the claim to the throne and was crowned King in June 1461.

EDWARD THE SEDUCER

EDWARD WAS A gregarious, charming and handsome man, who had one fatal weakness. He was very promiscuous and could never turn down a pretty face. Edward's love of pleasure and self-indulgent nature made him enemies, as did his propensity for selecting other men's wives as his lovers. His many mistresses bore him several illegitimate children, in addition to the ten children he sired with his wife, Elizabeth Woodville.

Sins of the Father

Edward IV took advantage of the confusion to snatch the throne for himself. Edward made a very different King than Henry. A marked contrast, the first Yorkist King was handsome, tall and brave, giving the country an inspirational and charismatic leader. Unlike Henry VI, he was also a strong leader, taking a guiding hand in policy making. But his usurpation was not enough to secure the throne. In 1470, Edward IV's cousin, Richard Neville, now known as Warwick the Kingmaker, sought power for himself and reinstated Henry VI, taking advantage of the King's timidity to rule in his name. Neville resented the fact that Edward did not listen to him. He also opposed Edward's marriage to Elizabeth Woodville in 1464, whose family helped themselves to titles and wealth that Neville saw as rightfully his.

Neville plotted to return Henry VI to the throne, as the King was by now even easier to dominate. Edward IV fled the country, seeking safety in Burgundy with his brother, Duke of Gloucester, only to return in 1471. Here, poor old Henry VI was sent back to the Tower and Edward IV triumphed over Neville and his army at Tewksbury. During this battle, Edward of Westminster was killed, meaning that Henry VI's only heir was now out of the picture. Soon after, perhaps as a result of the grief at losing his son or from the combination of events that had blighted the last few years of his life, Henry VI died during the night of 21 May. Rumors that Edward IV had ordered Henry's murder have never been proven.

Edward IV did not have long to enjoy his victory. His health started to fail and he died of a stroke in April 1483. Knowing he might die, Edward made his trusted brother, Richard of Gloucester, Protector of the Realm as his eldest son was only 12 years old (English Kings only reached their majority at the age of 18, from when they could rule unaided). Nevertheless, Edward was the rightful heir to the throne and was proclaimed King on 9 April 1483. But Edward V would never wear the crown. His loathsome uncle and Protector—who had been controlling the boy King from the word go—proclaimed himself King on 26 June, less than three months after the death of Edward IV, to whom he had sworn loyalty to Edward V. Richard III abducted the King and his brother, Richard, Duke of York, locking both boys in the Tower of London where they were rarely seen again.

FACT OR FICTION: RICHARD III

SHAKESPEARE PORTRAYS RICHARD III as a true villain. His physicality is monstrous to match his dark, conniving nature. Richard's anger at his deformity and the disadvantages it caused him have long been thought to be falsehoods added to embellish his ugly character. However, the discovery of Richard III's skeleton in Leicester in 2013 (see Chapter 1) has proved that Richard did indeed suffer from curvature of the spine.

... I, that am not shaped for sportive tricks,
Nor made to court an amorous looking-glass;
I, that am rudely stamp'd, and want love's majesty
To strut before a wanton ambling nymph;
I, that am curtail'd of this fair proportion,
Cheated of feature by dissembling nature,
Deformed, unfinish'd, sent before my time
Into this breathing world, scarce half made up,
And that so lamely and unfashionable
That dogs bark at me as I halt by them.

Shakespeare, *Richard III*

> Rumors whisper that Richard killed the unhappy princes to rid himself of the threat they might one day cause.

"Subtle, False and Treacherous"

Richard III is a captivating character who remains controversial to this day. The Tudor reign following his death helped to shape opinions of him as cheerfully murderous and capable of doing anything to secure the power he craved so much. Physically, his portraits show him to be a reasonably handsome man, if a little stern and knowing. Yet his iconic presentation in William Shakespeare's *Richard III* shows him to be disabled, even deformed—a hideous character both inside and out.

In art there lies some truth, which is that Richard would happily supplant his nephew Edward V and condemn him and his brother to a short and unhappy life in prison in order to usurp his throne. Rumors whisper that Richard killed the unhappy princes to rid himself of the threat they may one day cause. But the prized crown would not sit long upon his head. Two years of rebellion and suspicion would culminate

in Richard III dying in battle and the House of York losing the Wars of the Roses in favor of the descendants of Lancaster.

The bloody aftermath of the Wars of the Roses is one of the most fascinating in British history. Yet even the dramatic tales of bloodshed and treachery pale when compared to the antics of the Tudor family.

Right: Here we see Richard III in a classic portrait pose (head and shoulders at an angle). However, the painting shows nothing of the spine irregularity that afflicted the calculating King.

Anno 1505 octobis ymago henrici vii francoru3 rege illustrissimi
ozdinata p hermanni zinck Lo regie ... ailiarium .

HENRY VII: ORIGINS OF A DYNASTY

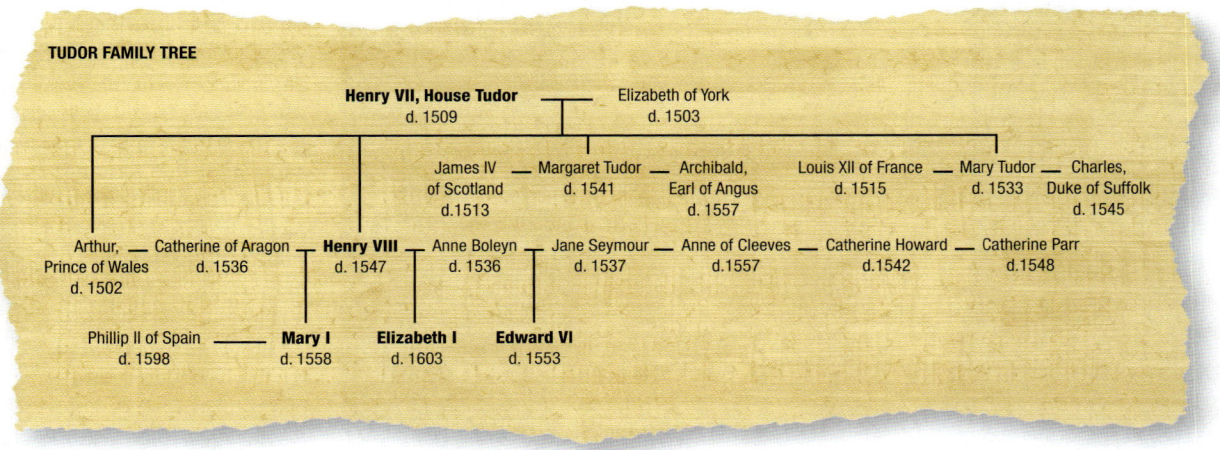

TUDOR FAMILY TREE

Henry VII, House Tudor
d. 1509 — Elizabeth of York
d. 1503

James IV — Margaret Tudor — Archibald,   Louis XII of France — Mary Tudor — Charles,
of Scotland   d. 1541   Earl of Angus   d. 1515   d. 1533   Duke of Suffolk
d.1513   d. 1557   d. 1545

Arthur, — Catherine of Aragon   **Henry VIII** — Anne Boleyn — Jane Seymour — Anne of Cleeves — Catherine Howard — Catherine Parr
Prince of Wales   d. 1536   d. 1547   d. 1536   d. 1537   d.1557   d.1542   d.1548
d. 1502

Phillip II of Spain — **Mary I**   **Elizabeth I**   **Edward VI**
d. 1598   d. 1558   d. 1603   d. 1553

The Tudor era lasted from 1485 to 1603. Compared to the House of Plantagenet (1154 to 1485), this was not long, yet the Tudor period is packed with some of the most famous and infamous British monarchs. Their legacy lives on in many dark and disreputable stories, including murder, execution, treason, false imprisonment, womanizing, illegitimate children, religious turmoil and the burning of heretics.

The turbulent reign of the first Tudor King, Henry VII, begins.

H enry VII's ascent to the throne in 1485 was by no means secure. At the time of his coronation there were more than ten others with a greater

Opposite: This picture shows King Henry VII, lavishly robed and holding a Tudor rose. Note the combination of the white rose of York and the red rose of Lancaster, united under the Tudor King.

claim than him, including his own mother, Margaret Beaufort. A direct descendant of John of Gaunt, Margaret was his great-granddaughter. However, a combination of circumstances, political manipulation and personal belief in himself as the rightful King would mean that Henry of Richmond would become Henry VII, the first Tudor King, who successfully ended the War of the Roses and united the houses of York and Lancaster. But his reign, and that of his ancestors, was by no means peaceful. Henry would live in constant fear of someone coming along to usurp his hard-won crown.

throne, so Henry was taken to Brittany by his mother and uncle, Jasper Tudor. Brittany was a separate, independent duchy, governed by Francis II and was at that time not considered part of France (even though the current French King, Louis XI, desperately wanted to claim it as part of his kingdom). This meant that Henry was relatively safe from attempts by both Edward IV, then Richard III, to coax Louis XI into sending Henry back to England, where it was likely that the threat he presented to the King would have resulted in his imprisonment or even execution.

During his time in exile, Henry grew up to be well versed in the ways of court and a noble life. As well as providing more traditional learning, his education would have included being able to ride, dance and pay a glowing compliment to the ladies of the court. However, alongside these frivolities lurked the

Growing Up in Exile

As Henry was a potential rival to the Yorkist monarchy—first to Edward IV, then Richard III—he was sent away from home for his own safety as a child. By the time Henry reached the age of 14 in 1471, his father, the weak-willed Edmund Tudor, had died and the continuing Wars of the Roses made life in Britain too dangerous for a potential claimant to the English

continuous threat that he, Margaret and Jasper might be forcibly returned to Britain.

Henry's long exile in Brittany did not end until 1485, when he chose to return to Britain with the aim of seizing the crown from Richard. Throughout his exile, both Edward and Richard had tried many times to rid themselves of the growing threat that Henry presented. It was the events in England that

THE TOWER OF LONDON

TODAY A POPULAR tourist attraction that houses the Crown Jewels, the Tower of London remains as a dark reminder of England's bloody past. Work on the Tower begun under William the Conqueror in the eleventh century, originally as a palace.

However, the Tower is most notorious for its use as a prison from the fourteenth century. It was here that any pretenders or challengers to the throne, plus anyone guilty of treason and awaiting execution, would be taken, occasionally to disappear forever (see the Princes in the Tower feature). During its long existence, the Tower has also been used as a fortress, armory, treasury and a home for the Royal Menagerie.

Below: The magnificent Tower of London still stands as a memory of England's bloody past. The fortress consists of several towers, including the Wakefield Tower, where mad Henry VI died in 1471.

followed Edward IV's death in 1483, then Richard's usurpation of the crown from his nephew, Edward V, that same year, which led to Henry's decision to seize control himself, which was both bold and foolhardy—a decision that would shape Britain's monarchy, political structure and religion for more than a century.

Reclaiming the Kingdom

A previous attempt in 1484 to snatch the crown from Richard, aided by the Duke of Buckingham (who had transferred his support from Richard to Henry), had been unsuccessful. Henry and his allies tried to land at Dorset but found Richard's troops waiting to strike. Henry returned to Brittany and Buckingham was executed while trying to escape to Wales. However, Henry would soon need to make another move. He

Above: His lunacy exacerbated by the stormy events of the past few years, Henry VI was captured during the Battle of Northampton in 1460. Due in part to Edmund Grey's treachery in refusing to fight against the Yorkists, the Lancastrians suffered a crushing defeat.

now had the increased support of other influential Lancastrian and Yorkist exiles, including his ever-faithful uncle, Jasper Tudor. Jasper ensured that Henry was kept safe throughout negotiations between Richard and Francis II, the Duke of Brittany. Francis initially harboured and supported Henry—despite Edward IV trying to get his hands on the boy—but he was not to be trusted and had secretly begun to negotiate with Richard ever since Louis XI's death in 1483. Henry and his exiles found out about this treachery and fled to France, where Charles VIII, the new young French

JASPER TUDOR

RELATIVELY LITTLE IS known about Henry's uncle, his father's brother, apart from the fact that he was one of Henry's greatest and most trusted advisors. Joining his nephew and sister-in-law in their exile, Jasper worked alongside Margaret Beaufort to promote Henry's claim and joined him in the decisive Battle of Bosworth. Jasper's allegiance came in part from his undying affection for his half-brother Henry VI, who had awarded him titles despite the dubious legitimacy of his parents' secret marriage. Jasper was also a skilled military man, his knowledge of battle tactics being put to good use at Bosworth Field. His reward was to be granted the title of Duke of Bedford in 1485, making him one of the only members of Henry's council to be of noble birth, in addition to Margaret Beaufort and John de Vere.

Right: Jasper Tudor (right panel) as depicted on a church stained glass window.

FACT OR FICTION: Y MAB DAROGAN?

A HUGELY INFLUENTIAL factor in Henry's Welsh support were the claims—highly exaggerated and played upon by Henry—that he was Mab Darogan, or the Son of Destiny.

Mab Darogan was a mythical figure in Welsh folklore who dates back to the time of King Arthur.

It was told that Mab Darogan would claim Britain back from the Anglo-Saxons, returning power to the Celts.

Henry's march through Wales and defeat of Richard certainly added flesh to the legend, and was a factor in both his victory and subsequent relations with Wales.

King, gave them sanctuary but offered little practical support to Henry in his claim to the throne.

The uncertainty of Henry's position, plus his growing support from men in France, England and Wales, meant that the time had come for him to make another attempt to appropriate the English throne. In addition to his ever-growing support, Henry had a stroke of good fortune when Richard III's only son and heir, Edward, died in 1484. His death left the path to the throne clear for Henry to take it for himself, casting off the Yorkist King once and for all.

Making His Move

Henry's decision to invade England via Wales was inspired; Henry's Welsh background meant that he could be sure of the support of several powerful Welshmen, including Rhys ap Thomas, an influential landowner and soldier who promised troops to Henry.

This time, Henry and his army sailed to Milford Haven, on the southwest coast of Wales. Landing in Wales to gather support enabled him to boost

his meager force of around 2500 men—made up of mercenaries and around 500 English exiles— giving him extra men to lead into battle against the might of Richard's superior forces. Despite being at a disadvantage, the second attempt proved much more successful, as Henry marched through Pembrokeshire to Shrewsbury, then on into the English Midlands. Richard, who had underestimated his own unpopularity and assumed that Henry's army would be opposed en route, was not as prepared as he should have been for a war on his own turf. However, his hastily gathered troops still far outnumbered Henry's army. He was aided in his war plans by John de Vere, the Earl of Oxford, who had deserted the Yorkists to lend his support to Henry and who would remain loyal to Henry throughout his reign.

Opposite: This illustration shows the imagined moment of Richard III's defeat at the hands of Henry VII at Bosworth Field, even though it is uncertain who actually dealt the blow that killed Richard. The new king is majestic and brave in this potent piece of propaganda.

DEEDS OF POWER: THE WELSH CONNECTION

HENRY OFTEN PLAYED upon his Welsh background when it suited him. He was born in Pembroke Castle in Wales, where he lived for the first four years of his life until he was taken to Brittany for his own safety. He named his first-born son Arthur, harking back to the Arthurian legends still strong in Wales.

He also made Arthur Prince of Wales in 1489, which did much to keep Welsh support, and celebrated St David's Day on 1 March. Henry also

kept up Welsh support during his reign by issuing charters giving certain Welsh communities the rights of freeborn Englishmen.

Of course, he made sure that he was well paid for any privileges he needed to award. Despite his championing of the Welsh when it suited him, Henry was actually only one-quarter Welsh. He never lived in Wales after his coronation and did not speak the language.

FACT OR FICTION: RICHARD'S REMAINS

AFTER THE BODY of Richard III was cut down from its gory display in Leicester—Henry wanted proof of his victory on display for all to see—he was buried in Grey Friars church in 1485, with Henry himself paying to have a monument erected. His body had at least ten stab wounds and it is not known who actually dealt the killing blow, although some bestow this honor on Rhys ap Thomas. But even in death Richard could not rest in peace. During Henry VIII's reign and the dissolution of the monasteries, Richard's body was allegedly tossed into the Stour River. A memorial on the site of the church was all that remained, until even that was covered over by various developments, the most recent of which was a car park.

However, in 2012 an archeological dig found both the memorial and a skeleton thought to be Richard's remains. DNA confirmed this theory in February 2013, so the question remains whether Richard will be either laid to rest in Leicester Cathedral or be returned to York as his final resting place.

Below: Excavated from beneath a car park in Leicester in 2012, the bones of Richard III clearly show the curvature of his spine.

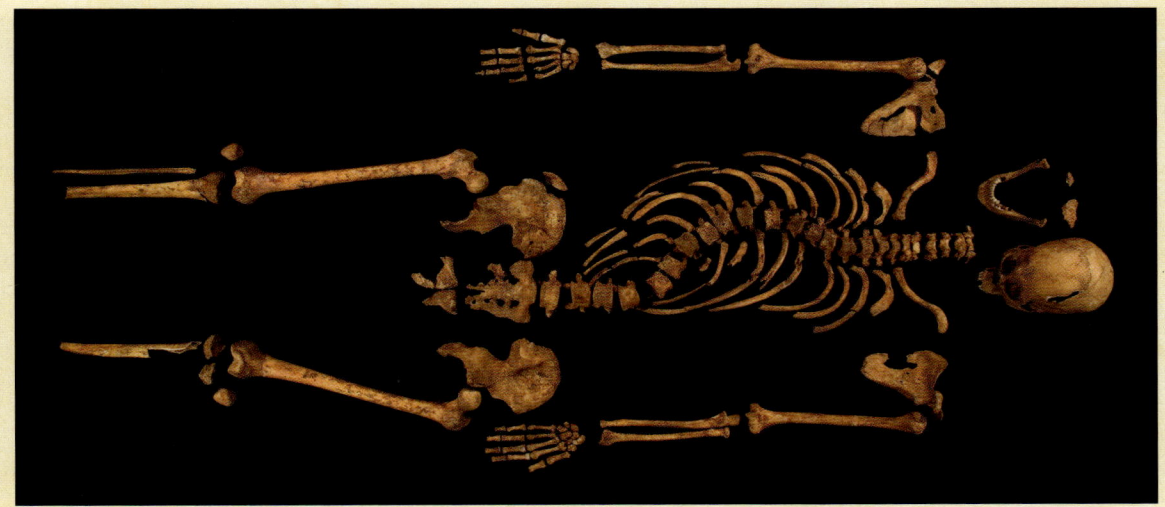

The Final Battle

Henry Tudor met Richard III and his troops on fields near the town of Market Bosworth in Leicestershire on 22 August 1485. Henry's army still numbered far fewer than Richard's and the outcome was by no means guaranteed. However, the Battle of Bosworth ultimately decided the fates of both men. This was largely due to the decision of some of Richard's supporters to turn their allegiance towards Henry in the midst of engagement. These included Thomas Stanley, Henry's step-father and Margaret Beaufort's third husband, and Henry Percy, the Earl of Northumberland, whose men first stood back and did not support Richard, then fought against the King, evening the odds on each side.

The last-minute change of support meant that Richard was now fighting a losing battle. Spurred on by this, Richard and 200 of his men made a desperate attempt to finish the battle by trying to reach and kill Henry himself. In this he was unsuccessful, despite

Opposite: After Richard III was struck down, his crown was retrieved and presented to Henry VII on the battlefield. This illustration shows Henry's men eagerly watching as they proudly hold Henry's standards aloft, surrounded by remains of the Yorkist troops.

> The unpopularity of Richard III meant that Henry's official coronation on 30 October 1485 was well received by the public ...

getting close enough to kill one of Henry's standard bearers. Richard was overwhelmed by Henry's supporters and killed on the field of battle, his army soon yielding. His death meant that Henry was able to claim the throne by right of conquest. Rumor has it that the crown from Richard's helmet tumbled off his head and rolled across the battlefield. It was later retrieved and placed upon Henry's head right there on the field at Bosworth by Thomas Stanley. History is told by the winning side, so how much truth there is in this version of events remains unknown. What is known is that Richard's corpse was stripped and displayed for his enemies to gloat over. Whatever the exact circumstances, the fact remains that Henry's victory was both a fitting end to his 14 years in exile and a dramatic start to a new age that changed the way the British monarchy, Church and government have been viewed ever since.

Consolidating His Power
The unpopularity of Richard III meant that Henry's official coronation on October 30, 1485 was well received by the public, but Henry left nothing to chance. He took every opportunity to safeguard himself against threats from usurpers. The right of conquest he had won on the battlefield was seen as the intervention of God choosing the rightful King, a powerful argument in itself. But Henry made no assumptions. He quickly called Parliament and made them declare that his reign had started from the day before the Battle of Bosworth. This meant that Richard's attempt on his life had been treason, but also that all those who had supported Richard were subject to charges of treason, too. They could all be executed if he desired, but Henry chose to save execution for the most troublesome ringleaders only. The rest were to be punished through fines and loss of lands, powers and privileges.

Henry also had his right to reign confirmed by Pope Innocent VIII. He made a triumphant and spectacular parade through the streets of London, winning public support. And significantly he started to appoint people who he knew he could trust to be his advisors. Here especially, he left no room for maneuvre, ensuring that these men were better off if they supported him, rather than if they made their own play for power. Another thing that helped Henry cement his leadership was that he was keen to make peace in England. Everyone was weary of years of fighting and hardship (war cost money through taxes and men who were needed to work to support their families). In Henry VII, people saw the chance for life to improve.

Leader of Men
While Henry had spent half of his life in exile (in fact he had never even lived in England, the country he was now to rule), he had been groomed for his role as King. His chaotic upbringing had naturally made him very suspicious of anyone in a position of power with a claim to the throne. However, he was a shrewd leader and soon began making decisions about his council, parliament and personal finances that made him feel more secure in his position. By surrounding himself with men who came from the gentry or the Church, as opposed to noblemen who—as history had proven—might start getting ideas about exploiting their powerful positions, Henry guaranteed their loyalty, making them dependent on his favor for money and support.

As well as his immediate family, Henry also rewarded trusted men who had been with him in exile, such as Bishop Richard Foxe (or Fox), an advisor and diplomat whom he made Lord Privy Seal, and John de Vere, whose military knowledge had proved vital at Bosworth and later at Stoke. De Vere was made Admiral of England, which was one of the most prestigious military posts at the time. Henry also surrounded himself with like-minded men who were eager to make themselves useful to their new King.

Uniting the Houses
A key point in making his throne more secure was his choice of bride. Henry was now able to wed his intended wife, Elizabeth of York. She was the daughter of Edward IV (the first Yorkist King of England) and Elizabeth Woodville and their marriage was intended to unite the houses of Tudor and York, putting an end to the Wars of the Roses. It would also give their heirs a far stronger claim to the throne than Henry ever had. Elizabeth was promised to Henry in 1483 after plotting

Above: Henry VII and Elizabeth, Edward IV's daughter, are married at Westminster Abbey in 1486. Henry made Elizabeth Queen Consort in 1487, uniting Lancaster and York.

His chaotic upbringing had naturally made him very suspicious of anyone in a position of power with a claim to the throne.

by Elizabeth's mother, Elizabeth Woodville, and Henry's mother, the redoubtable Margaret Beaufort.

Elizabeth Woodville had her own excellent incentive to see Richard defeated. As well as her daughter, Elizabeth had also been mother to Edward V, who Richard III had locked in the Tower and perhaps killed when he was just a child. Elizabeth Woodville's marriage to Edward IV, Edward V's father, was her second marriage. As she was related to the Lancastrians and was not of noble birth, the union caused much

controversy, especially when Elizabeth was crowned Queen Consort to rule at Edward's side. She still held some influence after Edward's death, despite derision for her low standing and habit of awarding her own family affluent titles. In 1487, Elizabeth left the court to spend the last five years of her life at Bermondsey Abbey. Speculation as to why she did this is that she hankered for a quiet, religious life. However, others believe she was forced out of the limelight by Margaret Beaufort, whose influence, especially over her son, was even greater than Elizabeth's.

As Henry and Elizabeth of York were third cousins, they had to get their marriage sanctioned by Pope Innocent VIII, which was readily done, making it an

MARGARET BEAUFORT

HENRY'S MOTHER, MARGARET, was a formidable woman who spent most of her life protecting him in exile, advancing his claim to the throne and then supporting him throughout his reign. Even though an act of attainder had been passed against her (meaning that she was liable to be executed for treason), she never stopped plotting on her son's behalf. Despite the fact that she had a greater claim to the crown than her son, she worked hard to ensure that his claim was strengthened in every way she could, displaying the same political savvy that her son would later show in compelling others' loyalty. With the help of Elizabeth Woodville, she arranged Henry's marriage to Elizabeth of York, thereby uniting the warring houses and putting an end to any remaining Yorkist threat against Henry.

In addition to the massive political benefits, the marriage arrangement was strengthened by Elizabeth Woodville's pledge of money and troops to support Henry's attack on Richard. Margaret would remain a leading influence over Henry throughout her life. She was also deeply religious, taking a vow of chastity in 1499 despite being married to Lord Stanley. Portraits of her often show her in prayer, despite her shrewd grasp of politics and willingness to remove anyone perceived as a threat.

Above: Elizabeth Woodville married Edward IV in the face of much controversy. Theirs was a secret love-match as opposed to a political alliance, which was more traditional for a king. Indeed, Edward was in talks to marry a French noblewoman at the time of his marriage.

> Henry had as his symbol the Tudor Rose, which shows the red rose of Lancaster enveloping the (smaller) white rose of York.

excommunicable offense for anyone to oppose their marriage or challenge either for the throne. They finally married on January 18, 1486 and Elizabeth was crowned Queen Consort on November 25, 1487. This, coupled with the fact that she had borne a son, Arthur, on September 20, 1486, meant that Henry's reign seemed far stronger than many other recent kings. To present this united front to his subjects, Henry had as his symbol the Tudor Rose, which shows the red rose of Lancaster enveloping the (smaller) white rose of York. However, the security that Henry craved still eluded him.

The Great Pretenders
As well as potential attacks from foreign lands, Henry had to deal with plots to usurp his throne from within his kingdom. The first significant assault on his right to rule came in the form of Lambert Simnel, a ten-year-old boy of humble birth. While Simnel alone would have posed no threat, he was in the hands of some very experienced and devious men. These included Richard Simon, an Oxford priest who was seduced by the thought of controlling a king. Simon tutored Simnel in how to act like a member of the aristocracy and was assisted by John de la Pole, the Earl of Lincoln (and Margaret Beaufort's first husband), who was in line to have succeeded Richard III had Henry not defeated him.

These men claimed that Simnel was actually Edward, the Earl of

Right: Pope Innocent VIII did not live up to his name. He bore two illegitimate children, granted indulgences to his supporters and encouraged war between France and Spain.

Warwick. Warwick was King Edward V's brother George's son, who had been imprisoned in the Tower of London and was thought to have died there. Rumors were spread that Warwick was alive and had managed to escape from the Tower. These claims were supported by the Earl of Kildare (Lord Deputy of Ireland), who was unlikely to believe the truth in these rumors, but was eager to invade England and support the vulnerable pretender. Henry tried to rubbish the claim by parading the real Edward, Earl of Warwick, through the streets of London to prove that Simnel was

Above: Elizabeth of York was seen as the perfect queen, being kind, caring and submissive. Henry VIII saw his gracious mother as a paragon to which his wives were unfavorably compared.

England to face Henry's forces at Stoke. This was unsuccessful, and on June 16 they were roundly beaten by Henry's men, whom he had prepared for a potential battle. Richard Simon was jailed for life—only avoiding death as he was a priest—and the Earl of Lincoln was killed in battle. Lambert Simnel himself was treated leniently. Henry gave him a position deemed fitting for someone of his birth— he was put to work in the royal kitchens, where Henry's supporters could keep an eye on him.

Four years later, in 1491, Perkin Warbeck appeared on the scene. He presented a far more serious threat to the throne. This time the pretender was a handsome 17-year-old servant who had a marked similarity to Richard, Duke of York, Edward V's brother. The Duke of York had also been locked in the Tower by Richard III. Their physical resemblance was noticed by Yorkists, would were naturally keen to push Henry off the throne.

Had the claim been true, Richard, Duke of York, would have had a stronger right to the throne than Henry. Warbeck's pretense still presented a problem for Henry, especially as he was supported by Margaret of York, Richard's aunt. She tutored Warbeck in courtly life and added truth to the lie by telling Warbeck all about the real Richard, which meant that his followers grew in number. As Simnel's earlier attack from Ireland had proved unsuccessful and the Irish were not keen to aid a second pretender, Warbeck and his supporters turned to Scotland for help. The

an imposter. However, Simon and Lincoln were not so easily dissuaded of their plans to become kingmakers and control a young monarch.

Events developed in Ireland on May 24, 1487, when Simnel was crowned King Edward VI, a move calculated to strengthen his claim in the eyes of his Yorkist supporters and the English public. The pretender and his puppeteers also garnered support from Margaret of York (the Duchess of Burgundy and a powerful ally), who arranged for 2000 troops to strengthen their cause. They then sent an army to

… in 1491, Perkin Warbeck appeared on the scene … This time the pretender was a handsome 17-year-old servant who bore a marked similarity to Richard, Duke of York, Edward V's brother.

Scottish King, James IV, was eager to lend support to anyone who could topple the English King, although how far he truly believed Warbeck to be Richard, Duke of York, is unclear. Yet his support was unwavering—he even pledged to wed Warbeck to a noblewoman from his own family—and the Scots invaded England in Richard's name in September 1496. As soon as James IV realized how unsuccessful and unpopular his decision had been he withdrew his support and returned. James IV later rid himself of Warbeck, sending him away on a ship aptly named *Cuckoo*, and made peace with Henry.

Warbeck refused to give up, turning next to the rebels in Cornwall who had been strongly opposed

Opposite: Henry VII is here pictured taking pity on the young pretender Lambert Simnel during his trial. It is thought that Simnel became a falconer after working in the palace kitchens.

THE PRINCES IN THE TOWER

RICHARD III FIRST CLAIMED that he sent Edward V and his brother, Richard, Duke of York, to the Tower for their own safety in the run-up to Edward V's coronation. It is rumored that Richard III arranged the murder of the two princes to prevent anyone thwarting his usurpation of the throne. In 1674, the bones of two young boys were found buried deep beneath a staircase. They were believed to be the lost princes and were laid to rest in Westminster Abbey. However, in 1933 when the bones were examined yet again, experts were no longer certain that these were the bones of the princes; rather, they might be just a few of the countless victims the Tower had claimed during the centuries it was used as a prison. The curious tale of the princes in the Tower remains a mystery.

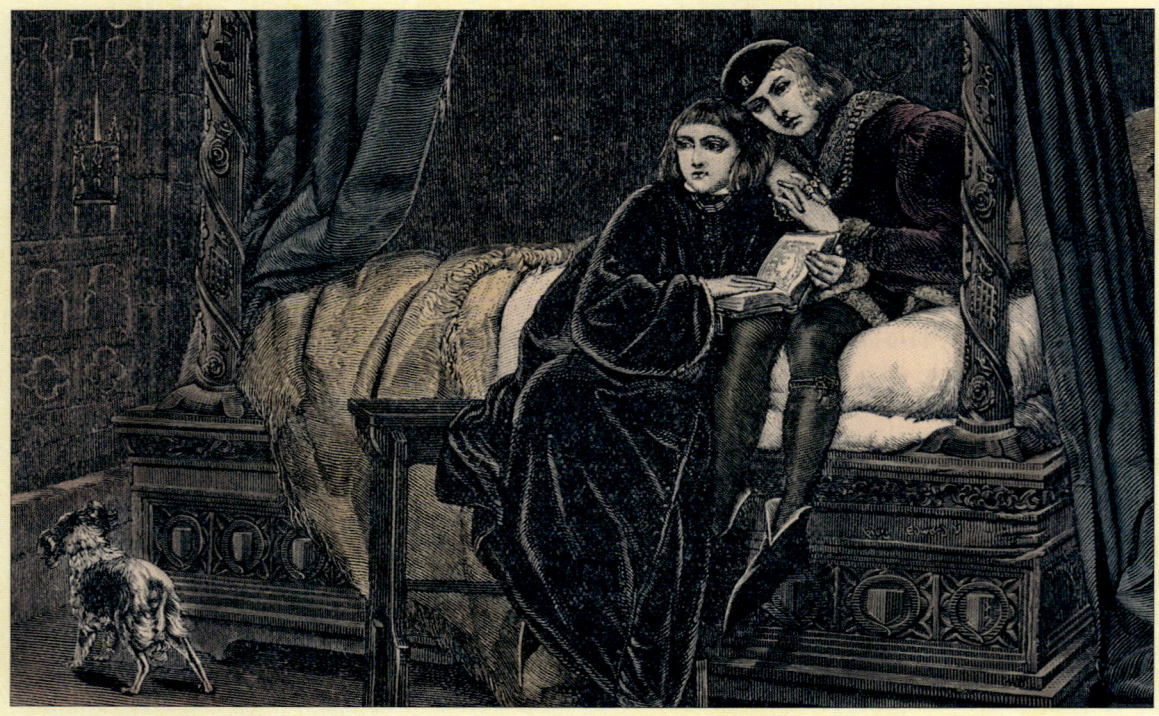

FACT OR FICTION: PRETENDER OR HEIR?

RUMORS STILL EXIST as to whether there was any truth to Warbeck's strongly asserted claims of being the real Richard, Duke of York, the rightful heir to the throne. While it is very unlikely that Warbeck was Richard, the resemblance he shared with his alleged father, Edward IV, means there was a chance that he was Edward's illegitimate son. While nothing was ever proven, Edward had several illegitimate children that are known about and possibly many more, so there may be a grain of truth in these rumors.

Warbeck fled but was soon captured and thrown in the Tower of London, after being forced to parade through the streets ...

to the higher tax collections needed for Henry to secure the north of England against Scottish invaders. Warbeck gained their support and he, together with an army of around 6000 men, made their attack. Once again they did not get far. Henry, due to his suspicious nature, had kept an eye on Warbeck's movements and sent his own forces to meet them at Glastonbury. Warbeck fled but was soon captured and thrown in the Tower of London, after being forced to parade through the streets of the capital, suffering the derision of the gathered crowds.

But Warbeck was a chancer and still his quest for power did not end. Imprisoned in the Tower, Warbeck joined forces with the real Edward, Earl of Warwick. The two men even managed to escape in 1499 but were soon recaptured and immediately put to death, Henry finally tiring of the threat that both posed and having good reason for the execution.

Fighting for Peace

With Warbeck finally dealt with, Henry resolved to further strengthen his own borders against any other potential threats. While Ireland would remain

Opposite: Henry VII was not as lenient with Perkin Warbeck as he had been to Simnel. Warbeck was first made to suffer public humiliation before his luck ran out. Henry deemed the pretender too dangerous to live and he was hanged on November 23, 1499.

a thorn in his side, he managed to make peace with Scotland. He and King James signed the Treaty of Ayton in 1497, which agreed peace between England and Scotland. It also stipulated that neither King could harbour a potential threat to the other King. To cement good relations, Henry also offered his daughter, Margaret, to James as his wife, thus further uniting the families. This union would later result in the Stuart family ruling England.

Margaret was only six when her father started discussing her marriage to James IV of Scotland, purely for reasons of political alliance. The couple were actually married in 1503, first by proxy on January 25, then on August 8 on Margaret's arrival in Edinburgh. This made her Margaret Queen of Scots. Despite it being a convenient alliance on both sides, James and Margaret were happy and loving, having six children together. Sadly, only one survived; James V, who became King of Scotland on his father's death in 1513. Margaret then became Regent of Scotland, ruling until her infant son could take over as King. However, she gave up this right when she remarried Archibald Douglas, Earl of Angus, in 1514. The Duke of Albany took over as Regent from 1515, taking control of James and his brother, Alexander until his death in December 1515. Margaret befriended Albany, only to take James back by force in 1524, where James was welcomed as the rightful King (under the guidance of advisors until he reached his majority at 18).

Mary's Marriages

Henry VII's other daughter, Mary, was also married for reasons of politics and the safeguarding of England. She was first betrothed to the Spanish Charles of Castile (who would later become Holy Roman Emperor), but in order to secure peace with France she married the French King, Louis XII, in 1514. He was 52 and she was merely 18 years old. Eager to produce an heir, they tried for children with vigor. Unfortunately for Louis, this brought about his sudden

MARGARET TUDOR

MARGARET TUDOR REMAINED an influential figure in politics, especially related to peace and cordiality between Scotland and England. Her personal life was tumultuous; she grew tired of her second husband's womanizing and political agenda and angled for a divorce. This was finally granted in 1527, whereupon Margaret took her third husband in 1528. She and her new husband, Henry Stewart, became James V's advisors and it was partly Margaret's influence that secured continuing good relations with England and her brother, Henry VIII. Her private life continued to cause scandal as she again applied for divorce, but this was refused by James V. Her control over James was diminishing although James' new wife, Mary of Guise, tried to reconcile them. Still married, Margaret died in 1541, reduced in standing and pining for England.

Below: Merely a teenager when she married the thirty-year-old King James IV, Margaret Tudor is shown here making the long journey to Scotland to wed her future husband. It was hoped that their alliance would unite the thistle and the rose.

> Just like his father before him, Henry VIII wanted his young, beautiful sister to make another marriage of alliance …

death just a few short months after their marriage. Mary did not fall pregnant before she was widowed and was glad to be rid of her much older husband.

Just like his father before him, Henry VIII wanted his young, beautiful sister to make another marriage of alliance, but she had fallen in love with Charles Brandon, the Duke of Suffolk. The two were married in secret in 1515. When Henry found out he was furious, first calling for Brandon's head as punishment for their disobedience. When he calmed down, he only made the couple pay a hefty fine for disobeying him. He was fond of his sister, but his affection for her waned when she opposed his divorce from Catherine of Aragon in favor of Anne Boleyn, whom Mary had disliked ever since Anne attended her wedding to Louis as maid of honor. Mary's granddaughter was Lady Jane Grey, who would briefly rule England on the death of Edward VI.

Threats from Overseas

Relations with foreign monarchs could be complicated. As in Britain there were often sudden changes in rulers, which resulted in dramatic shifts in alliances between countries. In addition to securing his borders, Henry cleverly avoided war with Charles VIII, when the French king forced Anne, the heir to Brittany, into marriage, thus making Brittany part of France under his control. Henry had promised support to Brittany, so in 1492 he sent troops to Boulogne. This was a clever move. It fulfilled Henry's bargain with Brittany and, as Charles was more interested in war with Italy than Britain, he wanted to avoid fighting on both sides of his country. The result was the Treaty of Étaples, securing peace between France and Britain. Charles also agreed to pay Henry and his army off with £250,000, a huge sum at the time.

Henry demonstrated his political proficiency once again by arranging a marriage between his eldest son, Arthur, and Catherine of Aragon, the daughter of Spanish King Ferdinand II of Aragon and Queen Isabella I of Castile. At that time, Spain was a superpower and it was in Henry's best interests to secure good relations. The marriage cemented their alliance, as did Catherine's later re-marriage to Henry VIII after Arthur's sudden death. This second marriage ensured that England and Spain remained allies, and also meant that Catherine's sizeable dowry remained in Henry's ever-growing coffers. Henry VII certainly took many steps to ensure peace and stability within England and with other countries.

Making Money

Despite his clever political alliances and peace treaties, Henry was never quite able to relax and enjoy his hard-won kingdom. He never forgot that there were many people with greater right to the throne than him. Henry's deep-seated distrust of the nobility grew throughout his reign and he worked hard to limit their powers and riches, while continuing to add to his own.

Henry VII inherited a country in debt from the many battles fought during the Wars of the Roses. He was also keen to live "of his own," meaning that he earned and spent his own money instead of directly taxing his countrymen for personal income. For a King this did not mean taking any sort of work. Rather, it meant making the most of financial loopholes that already existed for the monarchy. This was one area in which Henry and his advisors were experts.

Two of the most notorious of these advisors were Edmund Dudley and Richard Empson. They came from the gentry class, meaning that they were landowners and prominent, rich members of society. They were well-educated and ambitious, but generally did not have close ties to any of the nobility apart from Henry, meaning they were unlikely to have personal political agendas. As the burden of taxes and fines levied against the rich and poor alike worsened, stretching the borders of legality in every way, Dudley and Empson became more and more reviled.

Where the Money Came From

During his reign, Henry increased the value of crown lands and the rent earned from these lands by adding to them from the spoils of war. Anyone who was deemed a traitor to the crown lost lands and position, so any of Richard's supporters were stripped of all privileges. Another area ripe for exploitation was the King's "prerogative." This covered the profits from fines levied against feudal disputes and perceived

> ... in 1502 disaster struck. Arthur died suddenly from unknown causes ... just five months after his marriage to Catherine of Aragon. Henry was shocked and devastated by this sudden crisis.

injustices. The prerogative also included paying a fine on inheritance of lands and taxing the very rich on earnings. Any king could have made a profit from these fines, but Henry was one of the first to uphold their payments rigorously. In addition to raising money for himself, Henry was determined to keep a tight cap on the wealth of his most powerful citizens.

Customs duties were another area from which Henry profited hugely. London's port was always busy with merchant ships importing and exporting goods. Keeping the King happy meant the merchants could make a fortune, and even when Henry inflated the customs duties, the taxes had to be paid. Considering the vast wealth to be found abroad, it was in the merchants' interests to pay up, no matter how galling they found the high taxes. Henry also saved money by not investing in foreign wars (a huge expense that could result in crippling debts). All in all, Henry left his country a significant treasure.

It is a fact that his eagerness to make money made Henry VII unpopular with many rich and powerful men. This risk of making enemies conflicted with his desire to be as secure on the throne as possible and could have ended up with disgruntled nobles banding together to overthrow him, replacing him with a more sympathetic monarch.

Being an astute politician, Henry must have considered this. However, he made sure that there was enough capital to prevent an attack on British soil if one should occur. Henry's stockpiling hints at his underlying concern of one day experiencing the same type of uprising that enabled him to take back the crown from Richard. Having a surplus of funds at his disposal would mean that Henry could gather large forces at short notice, thereby safeguarding himself against potential usurpers.

Family Matters

Henry could feel secure about his ability to provide a male heir to the throne after his death. At the age of 39 he had fathered four children, two of whom were boys. His wife, Elizabeth, had provided him with the "heir and the spare." His first-born son, Arthur, would be King on his death. Henry also had another son, Henry, Duke of Cornwall, and two daughters, Margaret and Mary. Henry could feel confident that one of his sons would rule after him. As a bonus, he had two daughters who could be used to marry into political alliances, further strengthening the Tudor position. However, in 1502 disaster struck. Arthur died suddenly from unknown causes on April 2, just five months after his marriage to Catherine of Aragon. Henry was shocked and devastated by this sudden crisis. He was also perceptive enough to know that he could not depend on his one remaining son surviving him as King. Elizabeth, despite being 36 years old (a very late age to become a mother in Tudor times), became pregnant again, to both their joy. However, this joy was curtailed as the baby was a girl. Even greater grief was soon to befall Henry. His new daughter was stillborn and his beloved wife followed her within a few short days.

Henry did think of marrying again, even considering Catherine of Aragon for himself at one stage. Yet the anxiety of leaving only one male heir to the throne never quite left him. He was grief-stricken and weakened by Elizabeth's death, spending his remaining years keeping a close eye on his remaining son and heir, Henry, still under the influence of his mother, who even managed to outlive him by a few months.

Political Alliance Turned to Love

Henry and Elizabeth had been married for reasons of pure politics, but genuine devotion grew over time. It was their shared affection and their belief in

> Henry did think of marrying again, even considering Catherine of Aragon for himself at one stage. Yet the anxiety of leaving only one male heir to the throne never quite left him.

Cloth of Gold do not thou dispys
Though thou be mached with Cloth of fries,

Cloth of friez be not thou to bould
Though thou be mached with Cloth of Gold.

Trotter Sculp

Above: On the death of her first husband, the old and infirm King Louis XII of France, Mary Tudor intended to marry a man of her choosing. Mary is pictured here with her second husband, Charles Brandon, the Duke of Suffolk, whom she married in March 1515.

establishing a legacy that made them try for another child on Arthur's death. When this resulted in Elizabeth's death, Henry was said to be devastated. He gave her a grand funeral—sumptuous ceremonies being one of the few circumstances in which Henry was willing to spend lavishly—before she was buried in his tomb at Westminster Abbey, where he would join her on his death.

Opposite: Charles VIII of France married the fourteen-year-old Anne of Brittany in 1491, despite her being married by proxy to Maximilian I in 1490!

Henry: Man and King

Henry VII is generally far less well-known or infamous than his son. On his death in 1509 of tuberculosis, the crowds were believed to be jubilant that Henry VIII was to take his place. Opinions of him as a voracious, suspicious miser abound and he is often compared unfavorably to his heir—Henry VIII certainly looked

the part, more than his weaker, anxious-looking father, and was seen as a true King, to whom his subjects could look up to and admire. However, Henry VII also loved to enjoy himself. He liked to hunt, watch court entertainments, such as jesters, minstrels and dancers, and enjoyed gambling to the extent of it being almost an addiction.

Below: Henry VII writes to Ferdinand II and Isabella I about the forthcoming alliance between their children; Prince Arthur and Catherine of Aragon.

Opposite: Henry VII is pictured here with his advisors, Richard Empson and Edmund Dudley. Widely unpopular, they did not survive long after Henry VIII's accession in 1509.

Above: Only fifteen when he died, Arthur Tudor was never able to live up to his namesake, the legendary King Arthur. His brother, king in Arthur's stead, would become a legend himself.

Henry VII left behind the legacy of a rich kingdom, in contrast to the debts left by Edward IV (which Richard III had tried but not succeeded to wipe out). He put in place treaties to ensure peace between England and potentially threatening nations abroad. Henry also developed a law enforcement system that meant the fragmented arrangement following the Wars of the Roses was under tight control. Significantly, he left his remaining son a more secure throne than he ever had. However, both Henry VII's accomplishments and defeats have been largely overshadowed by Henry VIII's extraordinary personality and actions, and the sensational and scandalous Tudors who followed.

Above: Henry VII in his deathbed at Richmond Palace in 1509. The same mourners would soon celebrate his son's succession.

Opposite: Henry VII and his devoted wife Elizabeth of York lie together in their sumptuous monument at Westminster Abbey in London.

MARGARET AND MARRIAGE

EDMUND TUDOR, HENRY VI's half-brother and Henry VII's father, was Margaret's second husband, despite her marrying him as soon as she was of canonical age (12 years old). Her first husband was John de la Pole, to whom she was married in 1444 at the age of one! This marriage was dissolved in 1453 because Margaret was not of marriageable age and because she and de la Pole were related. Margaret was betrothed to Edmund even before her first marriage was dissolved and the two were married in 1455. Margaret was pregnant when Edmund died the following year, having contracted the plague while in captivity. Jasper cared for Margaret following his brother's death. Not surprisingly, Margaret saw Edmund as her first husband. She would go on to marry twice more after his death.

HENRY VIII:
BIRTH OF A LEGEND

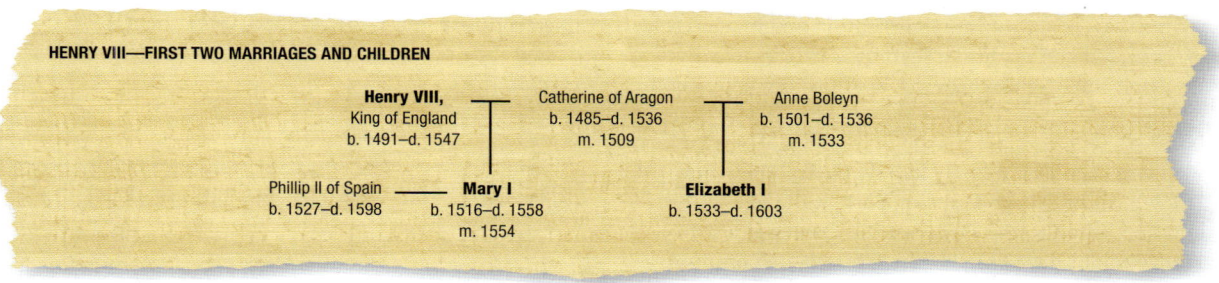

HENRY VIII—FIRST TWO MARRIAGES AND CHILDREN

Henry VIII,	Catherine of Aragon	Anne Boleyn
King of England	b. 1485–d. 1536	b. 1501–d. 1536
b. 1491–d. 1547	m. 1509	m. 1533

Phillip II of Spain	**Mary I**		**Elizabeth I**
b. 1527–d. 1598	b. 1516–d. 1558		b. 1533–d. 1603
	m. 1554		

For a young man with a healthy sense of self-worth raised as a prince, Henry had no trouble accepting his new role as King. Taking on the mantle of monarchy with ease, Henry's first and abiding priority was to make a strong, indelible mark on his kingdom. This was achieved beyond even his wildest dreams, making Henry VIII forever remembered as an autocratic, relentless and dynamic ruler. The most infamous King in British history had begun his 38-year reign.

"Kings of England in times past never had any superior but God."

The second son of King Henry VII, young Henry was born on June 28, 1491 at Greenwich Palace and groomed as a prince throughout his early childhood. His brother, Arthur, older than Henry by five years, would take the throne on their father's death. Henry was therefore allowed a slightly more informal childhood to the heir to the throne. Known for being a learned man, Henry was tutored under John Skelton, a Cambridge scholar who taught him the classics. Lord Mountjoy mentored him in how to act like a gentleman. William Hone tutored him in theology, a subject in which he became very interested. In this religious education were the roots of his later dispute with the Catholic Church. At the time of Henry's coronation and for almost 1000 years prior to that, Catholicism had been the only religion of England and much of Europe.

Opposite: Henry VIII is pictured here as an erudite, strong and handsome man. However, he is much more recognizable in his later portraits, where his large girth, jowls and humorless expression belie his poor health and temper.

Becoming Henry

Henry excelled at sports, loving horse riding, jousting, hunting and wrestling in particular. He was also well known for his dancing skills. In contrast to his father,

POWER OF THE POPES

THE POPE, HOLY Father or Bishop of Rome was traditionally the successor of Saint Peter, the first head of the Roman Catholic Church. By the time of the Reformation, the papacy was a wealthy and powerful institution. Centuries of corruption and hypocrisy had turned the office into a shambles, with indulgences being sold to those who could afford them enabling people to buy their way into heaven. Papal power was one of the key issues of reform.

Popes Leo X and Clement VII were cousins from the Medici family, an influential Florentine dynasty that produced four popes in total, using them to extend their power by controlling both council and church.

who was seen as a miserly killjoy, Henry knew how to enjoy himself. Made Duke of York at the age of three and appointed to the Order of the Garter at age five, Henry might have entered the Church—a common tradition for the second son—if his older brother, Arthur, had lived to be King.

But Arthur did not survive, and on his death in 1502 everything changed for Henry. In fact, the single event of Arthur's death—the exact cause of which is unknown—resulted in arguably the most significant event ever to affect the English monarchy, changing the entire country and causing death and destruction on a massive scale. Later that year, Henry was made Duke of Cornwall, then became Prince of Wales—a title that had previously been bestowed on Arthur—in February 1503. Now strictly supervised, Henry could not enjoy the freedom he had been used to. His father, Henry VII, was constantly worried that something would happen to his only remaining male heir, so Henry made few public appearances and had to limit his sporting activities. The young prince was almost always within view of his father or grandmother, Margaret Beaufort. He had to remain within the court and ask permission for everything, not even being allowed money of his own. As a strong and strapping young man used to being given whatever he wanted, this was very hard for Henry to accept. As soon as he became King, Henry would never again allow anyone to wield power over him. From the moment he was crowned, Henry was in charge.

Pleasing the Public

Despite a lack of kingly training compared to his brother, the public were delighted that the young prince Henry was to be the new King of England.

> In fact, the single event of Arthur's death … resulted in arguably the most significant event ever to affect the English monarchy …

Henry VII had done much for the country, including keeping the peace for much of his reign, but people were tired of the increasing demands for taxes used to build up the King's coffers. They were ready for change, and the handsome, dashing Henry VIII provided just that.

Henry VIII is well known for his bulky and imposing girth, unbending demeanor and grumpy expression, but as a young man he was slim, active, handsome and virile. He looked the part on his coronation on June 24, 1509 (Midsummer's Day), his six-foot-plus frame bedecked in jewelled robes of the richest velvet and the Imperial crown glistening on his head.

The previous day he had wed Catherine of Aragon, his brother's widow, in a simple ceremony. First refusing to marry her, Henry capitulated after Henry VII's death, saying that it had been his father's dying wish for the betrothal to take place. Henry's change of heart may also have been due to her generous dowry, which would have had to be returned to Spain with Catherine. The alliance with Spain that would be strengthened by the union was no small matter either, Spain then being a rich and mighty superpower in Europe.

Opposite: This is the marriage contract of Henry VIII and Catherine of Aragon. While the union was agreed in 1503, the couple did not marry until 1509.

Because Catherine had previously been married to Arthur, a papal dispensation needed to be granted by Pope Julius II, which Henry, at the time, declared himself happy with. This was despite Arthur himself claiming to have consummated the marriage with the memorable words "I have been this night in the midst of Spain."

Catherine had remained in England for the seven years since Arthur's death as Spanish ambassador. She was now 24 years old. A pretty, well-educated and deeply religious girl, Catherine felt it her duty to marry Henry. They were wed on June 23 and crowned King and Queen together in a spectacular ceremony at Westminster Abbey. Typical of Henry would be lengthy celebrations of splendor and extravagance, with entertainment, music, dancing and tables groaning under the weight of food and drink.

> Arthur himself claiming to have consummated the marriage with the memorable words "I have been this night in the midst of Spain."

Above: Catherine of Aragon did not have much luck with her marriages. Arthur died just months after they wed leaving Catherine adrift in a foreign country. It would be eight years before she finally married Henry VIII, at great personal cost and distress.

One of Henry's first acts after his coronation and marriage was an act of violence that cemented his decisive and ruthless reputation. It also showed the Privy Council who was in charge. In 1510, Henry ordered the execution of Richard Empson and Edmund Dudley—two of his father's most despised financial advisors—on the grounds of treason. Despite little or no corroborating evidence, Henry proved that his word was law and the men were duly executed, having very few supporters. Henry's propensity to execute anyone who stood against him or got in his way would become legendary throughout his reign. This bold move showed him as a force to be reckoned with—a powerful, unbending King who was unforgiving of mistakes.

Henry: The Lover

While ruling his court and country tightly, Henry returned to the "great matter" of providing the nation with heirs. Having seen for himself how precarious childhood was (as well as Arthur's death at 15, Henry lost two siblings who died in early childhood), Henry was eager to produce an army of male heirs. Catherine fell pregnant that year and gave birth on January 31, 1510. Delighted and proud that she had conceived so quickly, joy turned to disappointment at the miscarriage of a daughter. Quickly trying again, Catherine fell pregnant four months later and this time—on New Year's Day in 1511—she successfully gave birth to a baby boy. Henry was ecstatic and the whole country celebrated. Far from the anti-religious man he is sometimes portrayed as, Henry was deeply Catholic, regularly attending mass. He now gave thanks to God by taking the pilgrimage of Walsingham to the shrine of Mary to pray for his son and heir.

However, grief would soon follow joy. The boy, named after his father, died suddenly, destroying his father's delight and planting the first seeds of marital tension between husband and wife. While Henry was clearly able to father children, rumors abounded that Catherine was not so blessed.

Catherine fought against these rumors and finally, after several miscarriages, she gave birth to a healthy baby girl on February 18, 1516. Henry was pleased that she had managed to give birth, despite it not being the longed-for son, and they kept trying. However, Catherine was now 31 years old and unable to bear any more children. Henry, rumored to have had affairs during Catherine's troubles, now lost any sense of affection for his wife and no longer even tried to hide these from her or the court. The cruel King took up with the young and pretty Elizabeth (Bessie) Blount, with whom he had a son in 1519. That was the last straw for Henry's marriage. He was clearly able to have a healthy son, which meant that the problem lay with Catherine. Something had to be done.

Henry named the boy Henry Fitzroy and openly acknowledged his son, making the boy Duke of Richmond in 1525. He also started plotting to rid himself of his useless, barren wife.

Henry's mother, the lovely Elizabeth of York, had long been Henry's model for the perfect wife, mother and Queen. Fertile, loving and docile, Elizabeth had never defied Henry VII, a trait that he found most desirable. Henry's self-belief was so secure that he would find it hard to understand why people would not willingly submit to his every whim, dealing with those who stood up to him most harshly. Catherine would find this out soon enough.

Bessie was not Henry's first or last mistress. For a noble, having a mistress was expected, for the King it was almost encouraged. Henry—who enjoyed the chase as well as the feeling of falling in love—had several lovers and potentially several illegitimate children. His changeable and demanding nature made it difficult, even impossible, for any one woman to make him truly happy for any length of time. This same nature would mean his male advisors often fell out of his

favor, usually resulting in their execution. However, despite Henry being well-known for his six wives and numerous lovers, there were many other kings who were far more promiscuous, such as Henry's own grandfather, Edward IV.

Henry: The Fighter

Henry, while busy with affairs of the heart, was also busy with affairs of the state. He knew that the most successful kings grew their kingdoms and started trying to do exactly that. In sharp contrast to his peacekeeping father, Henry wanted the glory of war at any cost. While many of his advisors begged for restraint, others felt the time was right to press their advantage of the alliance with Spain. Ferdinand II, Catherine's father, was a willing ally, also wanting to strengthen his lands while weakening France. So it was, in the hot summer on 1512, that 18 English warships arrived in Spain. The plan was to join forces with Spanish troops and march into France across the Spanish border.

However, the deceptive Ferdinand had other plans. Happy to allow the English to guard the French border, he led his troops in a separate battle against Navarre in Spain. The English were left with no provisions, no shelter and no beer in the scorching Spanish sun. Disease quickly spread and there were many casualties. By October that year, the depleted troops headed for home, having achieved nothing apart from massive reductions in numbers and morale.

But Henry's lust for the heat of battle was by no means diminished. Furious at Ferdinand's betrayal—which he also partly blamed Catherine for—Henry joined forces with Maximilian I, the Holy Roman Emperor. In the spring of 1513 the English army went into battle once more. Sailing to Calais, followed later by the King, they laid siege to Therouanne in Flanders, taking the small town with ease. Pressing their advantage, they moved on to Tournai. The city fell after a week and Henry and his troops celebrated his victory as the great glory of England. Henry had proved himself a leader of men and a true, valiant King. Henry and his troops sailed home in triumph.

The cost of this war, however successful, was immense. Henry VII had left behind a fortune, yet

Opposite: Catherine of Aragon's father, Ferdinand II, is pictured here. Ferdinand and Isabella had six other children including Joanna the Mad, whose neuroses caused her to be held in solitary confinement.

Above: This picture shows the meeting between Henry VIII and Maximilian I, the Holy Roman Emperor, prior to the English invasion of France in 1513. Henry was desperate to win back France.

most of the excess had been gobbled up by Henry's desire to extend his authority. This meant taxes, which were never popular and which started discontented grumblings about Henry VIII. However, his victory in France, coupled with political events in England, meant that the charismatic King had the admiration and respect of most of his people.

Home and Away

England's ever-restless neighbor, Scotland, took umbrage at Henry's attack on their old ally, France. Taking advantage of the King's absence, in 1513 James IV led his troops over the border into England. Catherine, whom Henry left in charge as Regent in his absence, led the English against this uprising. At the Battle of Flodden Field the English quickly gained the upper hand, especially when James was killed after being hit by an arrow. The Scots were crushed and the victory complete. As a token of her love and admiration for Henry, Catherine sent him James' torn and bloodied coat (rumor has it that she also wanted to send his severed head!).

While one could argue that Henry's actual involvement in either combat was minimal—to say the least—both victories were won in his name and he was celebrated as the true, courageous King he always believed himself to be.

With Henry having proven himself in battle, there now followed a period of relative calm in England. In reality, this may have been down to the lack of funds

> The English quickly gained the upper hand, especially when James was killed after being hit by an arrow.

available for another war, but whatever the reason, England enjoyed the tranquility. All this was to change with the tumultuous and violent reformation.

With Henry's younger sister, the vivacious Mary, promised to King Louis XII, an uneasy alliance sprang up between the old enemies of England and France. This was due in part to Thomas Wolsey's diplomatic endeavours. Wolsey had been rising through the ranks of Henry's most trusted advisors for years. It was he who arranged the Field of the Cloth of Gold, a lavish meeting ground for Henry and Francis I, the new French King and Louis' cousin, in 1520. While the event was a

Left: Albrecht Dürer painted this likeness of Maximilian I in 1519, the year of Maximilian's death. Dürer also made woodcut prints of the egotistical emperor.

spectacle and celebrations, feasting and tournaments went on for two weeks, there was little progress in the good relations between the two monarchs. England's choice to support the stronger empire of Charles V was seen as treachery when Charles declared war on France in 1521.

Moving On

As King, it was no less than Henry's duty to provide his country with male heirs. This would be tricky while he was still married to Catherine, as any illegitimate children would not be able to enjoy a secure throne after his death. Henry also held little faith that his

TREATY OF LONDON

THE TREATY OF London was signed in 1518 after Charles V had become King of Spain on his grandfather Ferdinand's death. Signatories were the European nations of England, France, Spain, the Holy Roman Empire, Burgundy, the Netherlands and the papacy. Each superpower agreed not to attack any of the others and all would stand together if any faced an attack.

This raised England to being recognized as an important ally and European player, as it was because of the intercession of England that the treaty had been successfully signed.

Above: The Field of the Cloth of Gold was the site of an extravagant parley between Henry VIII and Francis I of France in June 1520. The dragon in the top left corner may then have been thought to be a portent, but was equally likely to be a flamboyant firework.

daughter, Mary—or indeed any woman—would be able to hold on to the throne. Henry had to remarry, and quickly. Turning to what he saw as the greatest weapon at his disposal—Catherine's previous marriage to his brother—Henry took action. Although she had sworn their marriage had never been consummated, which, for such a pious girl, was very likely the truth, Catherine and Arthur had been married for five months before Arthur's death and the prince had told his courtiers that they had been lovers. Henry was very familiar with the Bible from his religious education and grasped on to a passage from Leviticus, which stated that:

Henry was very familiar with the Bible from his religious education and grasped on to a passage from Leviticus …

And if a man shall take his brother's wife, it is an unclean thing: he has uncovered his brother's nakedness; they shall be childless.

Henry now had what he saw as the word of God that their marriage should never have taken place. Treating this as grounds for annulment—divorce being forbidden by the Catholic Church—Henry took his proof to the current Pope, Clement VII. An ecclesiastical court met in England to discuss the issue, but was recalled to Rome after two months, the

Above: Pictured here is Pope Clement VII. He forbade Henry's annulment, supporting Charles V—nephew of Catherine of Aragon and son of Joanna the Mad—over Henry.

CHARLES V

CROWNED KING OF Spain (then Castile and Aragon, plus kingdoms in Italy) in 1516, then Holy Roman Emperor and Archduke of Austria in 1519, Charles V became the most powerful ruler in Europe within the space of a few years. As heir to the Hapsburg, Valois-Burgundy, and Spanish dynasties, Charles retook parts of France as well as extending his empire throughout the New World. A fervent Catholic, he opposed Henry's break from the Church as well as the Lutheran reforms in Germany, eventually abdicating his thrones when his health failed. He had the famous "Hapsburg jaw" (see right), possibly caused by inbreeding.

matter still up for discussion. However Henry tried, he was unable to put enough pressure on the Pope, who was virtually a prisoner of Charles V, the Holy Roman Emperor and, unfortunately for Henry, Catherine's fond nephew.

Not one to let an insignificant person like the infallible head of the Church tell him what to do, Henry persevered in getting the annulment he so desired. This would lead to him defying the Church he once believed in so devoutly and becoming supreme head of the Church of England in 1534. Henry's motives were led by his growing lust for another woman, plus what he saw as his kingly duty in

> Henry's motives were led by his growing lust for another woman, plus what he saw as his kingly duty in providing a male heir …

providing a male heir for England after his death. But Henry had not expected to face the combined refusal of both the clergy and Catherine. Her stubborn nature now revealed itself and her strict Catholic upbringing meant that divorce was not an option for her. Catherine refused to acquiesce to Henry's demands. The fact that she would have to leave England in shame also played a part in her defiance. While some sympathy was with Henry for naturally wanting a son, most sided with the wronged Queen against the lascivious King and the object of his fancy, Anne Boleyn.

Marriage Wrecker, Church Breaker

Anne was the daughter of Thomas Boleyn, one of Henry's favorite diplomats. She attended Mary Tudor after her marriage to Louis XII at the French court.

> While some sympathy was with Henry for naturally wanting a son, most sided with the wronged Queen against the lascivious King

Described as accomplished, opinionated and witty, she drew the eye of the King soon after being recalled to the English court in 1521. Anne, knowing that she had attracted Henry's attention, played her part carefully for years, flirting with him and making her interest clear, but never overstepping the grounds of propriety. Anne refused to settle for being merely a mistress, like so many before her. She often withdrew from court to spend time at Hever Castle, her childhood home, but kept up a correspondence with Henry so that she was always in his thoughts.

A lover of courtly romance, Henry sent Anne letters, poems and tokens of affection. The lengths he was prepared to go to in order to marry Anne shows the thrall she had over the amorous King. An ambitious and intelligent girl, Anne held out for

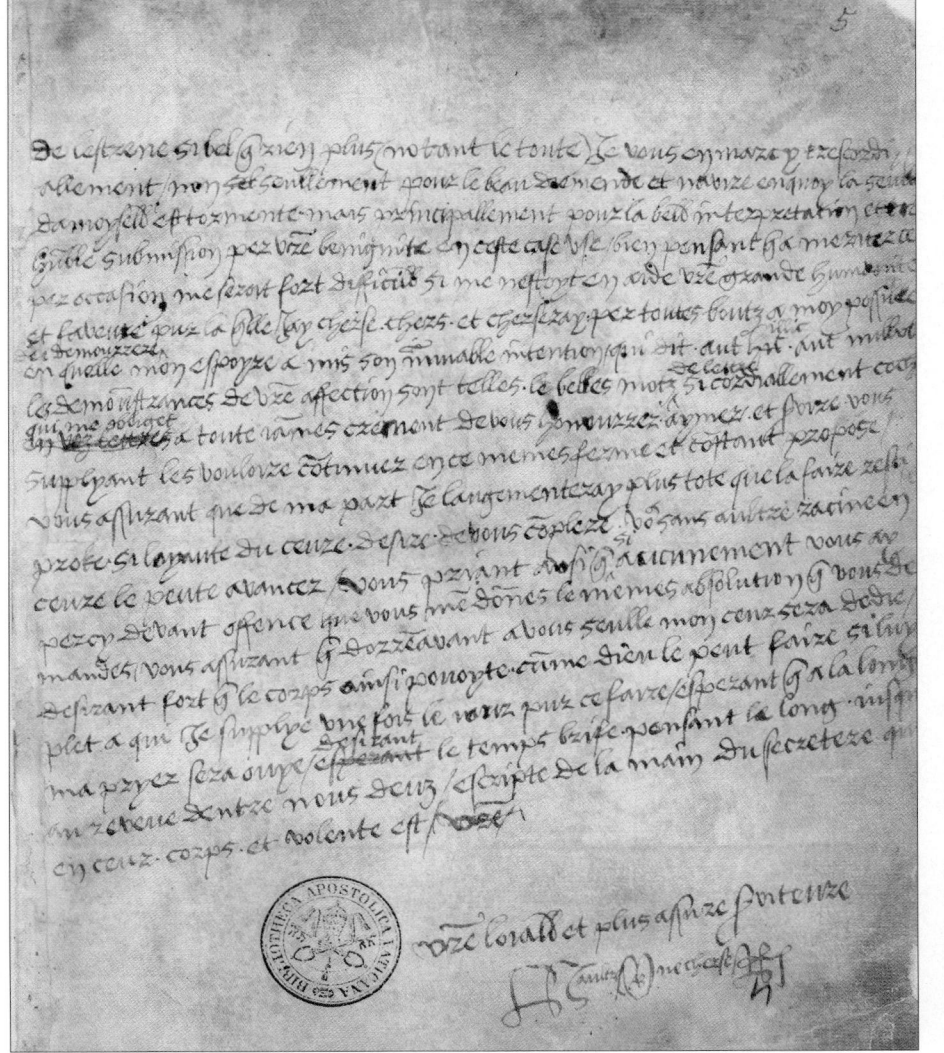

Left: A love letter from Henry VIII to Anne Boleyn, circa. 1528, when Henry was still hoping for an annulment from Rome. The romantic King writes that his "heart will be dedicated to you [Anne] alone."

THE OTHER BOLEYN GIRL

PRIOR TO MARRYING Anne, Henry had enjoyed the favors of her elder sister, Mary. Both girls had spent time in the French court of King Louis XII, where they had learned the arts of coquetry and seduction. Mary had been Henry's mistress for around five years after leaving the French court amidst rumors of a possible affair with Francis I (Louis' successor) and several other courtiers. However, it was Anne that Henry married, after she drove him to distraction with her flirtatious ways.

A scandalous rumor spread around the court that Henry had bedded both sisters and their mother. When Henry was told of this, his response was "Never the mother!"

Left: The British artist William Hogarth painted this picture in the eighteenth century. Entitled "Henry VIII (1491–1547) introducing Anne Boleyn at court," we see a besotted-looking Henry guiding Anne towards a doubtful—and perhaps concerned—Cardinal Wolsey.

Opposite: This illustration depicts Thomas Cranmer, the man who married Henry and Anne after announcing the King's first marriage null and void. Becoming Archbishop of Canterbury in 1532, Cranmer was executed in 1556 by Catherine's daughter, Mary I.

the prize of being Henry's Queen and would not settle for anything less. Henry even made Anne the Marquess of Pembroke, the first woman to ever have been given a peerage in England. His devotion to making Anne his Queen was clear, despite the majority of public sympathy being firmly on Catherine's side and the disloyal Anne being widely unpopular.

Above: Taking his revenge on Pope Clement VII for not permitting his annulment, here Henry VIII is seen trampling on the Pope. The message is clear; Henry now answered only to God.

In 1531, Henry decided that enough was enough. He had lived a virtually separate life to Catherine for over a year and Anne was still holding out on him.

RELIGION IN ENGLAND

ENGLAND UNDER HENRY had always been a devoutly Catholic country. (Henry himself had even been titled Defender of the Faith in 1521, when he attacked Luther's reforms.)

Most people went to weekly mass and prayed, often to icons of Jesus and Mary or the cross. People prayed to icons of saints and the holy family, and transubstantiation (the symbolic bread and wine given out during the mass being turned into Christ's body and blood) was believed to be fact. Anyone who disputed this could be accused of heresy.

Perhaps Henry's biggest achievement—if you can call it that—was managing to adapt such orthodox beliefs to a new faith.

Because Charles V had virtual control over the Church and Pope, there was no way that an annulment from Catherine, Charles' aunt, would be permitted.

Tired of waiting for other people to decide his fate, he banished Catherine from court and set Anne up in the Queen's quarters. In 1533, he and Anne were married in secret, despite Henry still being legally married to Catherine. Anne quickly fell pregnant, which Henry saw as proof that he had made the right choice, whatever the

Right: Pictured here, Martin Luther shared Henry's dislike of the papacy, but for different reasons. It was Luther's abhorrence of the idea that one could buy one's way into Heaven that prompted his split from the Catholic church in 1517.

consequences. This meant they had to seal the deal and a second, official wedding took place on January 25, 1533. Shortly after, Thomas Cranmer, who had recently been appointed Archbishop of Canterbury after the uncooperative Archbishop Warham died in 1532, performed the ceremony and also presided over a court of clerics that ruled Henry's marriage to Catherine as officially null and void. Catherine was given the title of princess dowager on account of being Arthur's widow and the triumphant Anne was crowned Queen Consort on 1 June.

Splitting the Church

The complex business of the English reformation and break with the Catholic Church of Rome was credited as being a result of Henry's desire to marry Anne Boleyn. While this was certainly the catalyst, Henry's political manoeuvrings and eye for power may well have resulted in this breach happening sooner or later. Because Charles V had virtual control over the Church and Pope, there was no way that an annulment from Catherine, Charles' aunt, would be permitted. If the

THE FIRST REFORMER

MARTIN LUTHER WAS a German monk who first began stirrings of discontent within the Catholic Church in 1517. He was strongly opposed to the selling of indulgences to ensure your soul went to heaven after your death, no matter how much you had sinned. Luther also wanted to do away with some of the sacraments that mystified religion and make it accessible for every man and woman who believed in Jesus Christ, no matter how poor they were. Luther felt that the Church had lost sight of its origins and he wanted to return to a purer religion based on faith. Immediately condemned as heretical, Luther was excommunicated by Pope Leo X in 1521. His reforms became widely known all over Europe (thanks to developments in printing) and were discussed in many universities, including Cambridge. His translation of the whole Bible into German, making it accessible to everyone, was published in 1524.

head of the church would refuse him, Henry, believing himself to be right, felt he had no other option than to take control of the church himself. More so than any other monarch, Henry VIII truly believed himself to be God's representative on earth, answerable only to God with authority that outranked even the Pope.

Henry began attacking the Church. He first reintroduced the law of *praemunire,* which meant that anyone supporting papal bulls or jurisdiction (which had been classed as a foreign power and therefore against England) was acting against the monarchy. The sentence for this was death. The Submission of the Clergy meant that church laws could only be made with permission from the King in case any religious acts were contrary to those made by the monarchy. Similarly, the Supplication Against the Ordinaries further removed church powers. The Absolute Restraint of Annates Act meant that people were forbidden to send money to the Pope. The title of Pope was replaced with Bishop of Rome. Slowly but surely, Henry was stripping away the power of the Church and replacing it with his own power. In 1534 Henry drove another nail into the coffin of the Catholic Church. He announced the Act of Supremacy, by which Henry officially broke with Rome and became Supreme Head of the Church of England. The Act states that:

… the Kings Highnesse is the onely Supreame Governour of this Realme, and all other his Highnesse Dominions and Countries, as well in all Spirituall or Ecclesiasticall things or causes …

… and goes on to ask for allegiance to the King only. The Act is often seen as the beginning of the reformation, although by taking steps towards this final action and using Parliament to announce the Acts, Henry cleverly made it appear to be what

Opposite: The Battle of Pavia between Spanish-Imperial troops supported by England against the French largely decided the Italian Wars of 1521–1526. Francis I was captured by the Spanish and forced to surrender. This picture shows Charles V's troops rapidly advancing.

ERASMUS

DESIDERIUS ERASMUS OF Rotterdam was a humanist and Catholic priest who translated the bible from its original into Greek and Latin editions. He was a leading influence of Luther and other reformers, but never personally took such a strong line. A confirmed Catholic, Erasmus wanted to stop misdemeanors such as paying for indulgences and corruption within monasteries. He made no attacks on the Church and did not support Luther, despite the monk asking for Erasmus' commitment, for fear of the violence and disarray he thought the Reformation would bring.

England wanted. This was no easy feat in a country that had been Catholic since Medieval times. While for many this change was in name alone, there was a gradual shift away from the worship of deities, icons and shrines that had been an integral part of everyday religious life.

Typical of Henry, the King also introduced the Treasons Act, making it punishable by death to refuse to swear the Oath of Succession, which stated that any children he had with Anne were the rightful heirs to the throne. As well as gaining power, Henry would gain capital. A huge source of income, the Church was paid taxes with which to keep the monastic houses afloat. Cromwell was significant in the *Valor Ecclesiasticus,* a survey of how much wealth and property was owned by the Church. Henry began to tax the Church on the basis of this survey—a tax of up to ten percent of all earnings. The Reformation Parliament covering these Acts ran from 1529–1536. Officially nothing to do with Henry's marital status, it started as a hunt for sins against God within the monasteries, such as adultery, homosexuality, theft and drunkenness. Henry also ordered that all monastic houses of less than £200 ($284.25) a year were to be closed. The dissolution of the monasteries had begun.

Despite his split from the Church and destruction of the monasteries, Henry remained to his last a devout man, fully believing most Catholic theology. While his reforms led to much bloodshed, it could be said that Henry aimed to keep the origins of Catholic faith while stripping away its vanity and superstitions. However, one must not forget that he had a personal investment in the reformation and profited handsomely from it. Henry VIII was excommunicated by Pope Paul III (Clement VII's successor) in 1538.

All the King's Men

Thomas Wolsey first entered Henry VII's court as Royal Chaplain. On Henry VIII's coronation he became an almoner (a distributer of alms or money to the poor). By a mixture of personal ambition, charisma and diplomacy, Wolsey quickly rose to be one of Henry's most powerful advisers. His rise was also aided by the fact that Henry had little interest in the detailed ins

Opposite: Thomas Wolsey is shown here in his distinctive red Cardinal's robes. He became Cardinal in 1515, as well as being Henry's chief advisor until his downfall.

> Despite his split from the Church … Henry remained to his last a devout man, fully believing most Catholic theology.

Above: Pope Paul III finally excommunicated Henry in 1538. Having gone against the Catholic Church many times, the final straw was when the shrine of St. Thomas Becket of Canterbury was destroyed that same year during the dissolution of the monasteries.

and outs of administration on which his father had kept a close eye. Henry VIII insisted on making all of the decisions, but he wanted things presented to him simply rather than spending hours bogged down with bureaucracy. Careful to follow the whims of the King, Wolsey adapted his anti-war position when he saw that Henry was determined to wage war on France.

Wolsey's flexibility and diplomacy aided his rise from a member of Henry's Privy Council to Lord Chancellor in 1515, as well as Archbishop of York, then Cardinal, although many others were not happy that a commoner had been given so much influence. Prominent in both the council and Church, Wolsey's diplomatic skills were tested and proved competent during negotiations with France. If there was to be war, Wolsey would make sure it was won by the English. Learning from the first abortive attack on France in 1512, Wolsey made sure that England's second attempt to win back French territory in 1513 was successful. The men were properly housed and fed, enabling them to fight well. Following England's victory at Tournai, Wolsey successfully negotiated peace with France, whereby Louis would marry Mary and England would keep the hard-won city of Tournai.

LIVING LIKE A KING

WOLSEY HAD ALWAYS liked the finer things in life and was responsible for some fabulous properties being built—Hampton Court in particular. Begun around 1514, Wolsey rebuilt the existing manor into an extravagant pleasure palace, with rooms for the royal family as well as himself. Foreign ambassadors would visit and the aim was for them to be awed by the splendor of such a rich and beautiful establishment. Henry took over the palace in the late 1520s, changing and adding quarters. By the time he died in 1547, Henry owned over 60 properties, but Hampton Court Palace remained his favorite.

Above: Here we see the opulent Hampton Court Palace from the opposite bank of the River Thames. Henry spent a lot of time at Hampton Court, which appealed to his love of Renaissance architecture. He extended the Palace in this style.

Perhaps one of his most delicate tasks was to make alliances between England and France and England and Spain at the same time. With Charles V now ruling a large section of Europe, and leading a war against France, it was now in England's best interest to strengthen this alliance. Henry tried to take the French crown back for England when Francis was captured during the Battle of Pavia in 1525.

Henry was eager to invade France once again, but previous attempts had yielded little and cost a lot. Suffering from a lack of funds, Wolsey tried to raise money for his power-hungry King. He set up a highly controversial tax called the Amicable Grant in 1525. Despite its name and being called a benevolence, it was basically an enforced loan to the Crown. Wolsey did not have the backing of Parliament, so the Grant

Trying to curry favor, Wolsey gifted Henry his home of the sumptuous Hampton Court Palace.

was unstable from the beginning. The theory was bad enough, but in practice it was a disaster. Riots were violent and widespread. In the face of such enormous opposition, Henry had to back down. Claiming that the Grant had not been his idea, he left Wolsey to clean up the mess.

His many enemies loved seeing him out of favor, but Wolsey managed to save his job and neck. Trying to curry favor, Wolsey gifted Henry his home of the sumptuous Hampton Court Palace. The Cardinal then worked tirelessly to secure the annulment for Henry to escape his marriage to Catherine, but his pressure on the Pope was not as threatening as Charles V's. Wolsey was unsuccessful and Anne Boleyn struck another nail in his coffin when she turned against him. Believing him of deliberately delaying the King's annulment, Anne and the Cardinal's many enemies plotted against him, leading to his arrest in 1530.

However, despite such an extravagant gift from his loyal servant, Henry ordered Wolsey to be sent to the Tower to answer claims of treason. On the journey, the stress of trying to please his thankless King grew too much for the Cardinal and he died on November 29, 1530.

The Pious Man

A friend of Erasmus, Thomas More was a pious Catholic who was tormented by his King's treatment of the Church. A supporter of anti-Lutheran movements, he was wholly supportive of the sacraments and traditions of the Church. Beginning his political career as a lawyer, More became a member of Henry's Privy Council in 1514. He worked closely with Cardinal Wolsey, becoming under-Chancellor of the Exchequer and Speaker of the House of Commons. On Wolsey's fall from grace, More became Chancellor himself. A loyal supporter of both the King and the Church, More first stood behind Henry's actions, trusting in his King. He tried to stamp out the Lutheran uprisings, aiding Wolsey in preventing Luther's books being published or

read in England. More was also responsible for six men being burned at the stake for heresy during his time as chancellor.

Increasingly uncomfortable with the King's actions, More did not support Henry's plan to annul his marriage to Catherine. While he did support the Act of Succession, More tried to resign from the court

Opposite: Added between 1532– 1535, Hampton Court's Great Hall is a magnificent reminder of Henry VIII's extravagance. Used for ceremonies and celebrations, it could hold the entire royal court.

> Increasingly uncomfortable with the King's actions, More did not support Henry's plan to annul his marriage to Catherine.

and withdrew his ardent support for Henry. His long-standing service and influence could only save him so far. More signed his own death warrant when he refused to attend Anne Boleyn's coronation. Matters came to a head when he steadfastly refused to swear an oath declaring Henry to be supreme head of the church. He also refused to support Henry's annulment of his marriage to Catherine. A steadfast believer in order and tradition, More was not able to accept that one man, even if that man was King, could replace the entire hierarchy of the church.

Taken to the Tower, More stood trial in July 1535 where he was found guilty of high treason. His sentence was to be hanged, drawn and quartered, but this was reduced to the slightly more palatable sentence of beheading. Despite contrasting accounts of his character, it is clear that he was a devout Catholic who was prepared to die for his faith. More was canonized as a martyr in 1935.

The Bishop

John Fisher was the chaplain and confessor of Lady Margaret Beaufort, Henry VII's mother. It was with his help that she founded

Left: This picture shows Thomas More, who rose to powerful heights under Henry VIII before refusing to renounce the Church in favor of Henry's supremacy.

PROFILE: A MAN OF ENIGMA

MORE IS FAMOUS for writing the influential *Utopia* (1516), meaning "good place," a book that compares life in England to an ideal society based on communist principles, widespread peace and rational thought. Religious tolerance also features highly. This ideal society of tolerance is at odds with persisting rumors about the austere and strict More using violence and torture against those accused of heresy, which contradicts his veneer of a virtuous and moral man.

Whatever the truth, More never admitted to using torture and appeared to be against the deaths caused by heretical propaganda, leading to the barbarous German Peasants' Revolt in 1524–1525.

> It seems that Cranmer lived through Henry's reign and into Edward and Mary's reigns due to his moral flexibility.

some of the Cambridge University's colleges. He became Bishop of Rochester in 1504 on Henry VII's insistence and was one of Henry VIII's tutors. A learned, articulate man, Fisher was anti-Lutheran and supported Henry's fight against heresy, wanting to return to a more traditional Catholic faith. Despite their long relationship and common beliefs on religion, it was when Henry took steps to divorce Catherine of Aragon that Fisher could no longer support his King.

Even after attempts were made on his life, Fisher was not put off his beliefs. Refusing to swear that Anne's marriage to Henry was valid and that their heirs would be legitimate, Fisher was sent to the Tower on April 26, 1534. Pope Paul III tried to intervene by making Fisher a cardinal. But Henry was not to be moved and sent back the message that Fisher's head would be off his body before the red cardinal's hat was on his head.

Various attempts were made to trick Fisher into condemning himself by speaking out against the King, but he kept up a dignified silence until Richard Rich, a solicitor general who worked under Cromwell,

Opposite: More is shown in a final embrace with his daughter, Margaret Roper, just before his execution at Tower Hill. Margaret married the biographer William Roper, whose account of his father-in-law described More as a man of "clear unspotted conscience."

tricked Fisher into admitting his disbelief that Henry was the supreme head of the Church. Rich spoke out during the trial, leading to Fisher being found guilty of treason. As he had been stripped of his bishopric, Fisher would have been hanged, drawn and quartered if it weren't for the massive public support he was gathering. He was subsequently beheaded at Tower Hill on June 22, 1535. His body was ignominiously stripped and thrown into a grave with no proper burial and his head was hung from Tower Bridge. Also canonized, Fisher shares the feast day of June 22, with Thomas More—two men who died for their religion and refused to let any man destroy their faith.

The Survivor

Instrumental in the annulment of Henry's marriage to Catherine of Aragon, Thomas Cranmer opened the court for the King and Queen to present their cases. He judged that Henry's marriage was against God's law on May 24, 1532. On May 28, Cranmer validated Henry's secret marriage to Anne and he also presided over her coronation on June 1. In addition, on September 10, Cranmer became godfather to Elizabeth (as he had been to Edward), his future Queen. Cranmer was Archbishop of Canterbury by this time. It was also Cranmer who declared Henry's marriage to Anne null and void shortly before her execution for treason. It seems that Cranmer lived through Henry's reign and into those of Edward and Mary due to his moral flexibility.

Cranmer had been a lecturer of divinity at Cambridge until he said that Henry could get out of his marriage to Catherine if it could be proven that she had consummated her marriage to Arthur. The Prince's words of being "in Spain" would come back to haunt Catherine.

Cranmer also spent time in Germany consulting the Nuremberg princes on a religious alliance between Germany and England. His Bishop's Book of 1537 aimed to implement the Ten Articles and the reforms made to the church so far, while bridging tradition and reform. While these reforms modernized the Church of England, they did not go as far as Lutheran principles, some of which were still regarded as heresy.

While Cranmer gained himself the typical enemies of anyone with influence in the Tudor court, Henry remained attached to him, even when Cranmer's ideas on reform went further than the King's. Cranmer was never ambitious for more power and always went along with his King, which was probably a big part of Henry's affection for him. It was Cranmer who Henry asked for in his final hours, perhaps the closest thing to a friend he ever had.

The Politician

First entering Wolsey's service in 1524, Thomas Cromwell quickly proved himself useful by aiding in the dissolution of 30 monasteries in order for Wolsey to fund schools with the profits. Cromwell then joined Wolsey's council and was one of his most trusted advisors by 1529. However, things began to look shaky for Wolsey around this time, so Cromwell quickly distanced himself from Wolsey's unpopular decisions. He managed to stay in favor with Henry, becoming a member of the King's Privy Council in 1530. But, by this time, Cromwell had made enemies of his own.

Below: John Fisher was executed only weeks before Thomas More. This illustration shows that Fisher was beheaded, having been spared a more agonizing and drawn-out death (note the gallows and burning stake behind him, both of which are occupied!).

> ... the King's marriage to Anne now formalized, Cromwell aided him in weakening the Church in order to discredit the institution ...

His actions in aiding the King's divorce from Catherine of Aragon and the position of royal supremacy added to his enemies. These were men who disagreed with him over Henry's disquieting actions and those who were uncomfortable with the amount of power Cromwell could now wield. But Cromwell seemed to be untouchable. In 1531–1532, he led the Reformation Parliament to support the King's royal supremacy on the grounds that the church and clergy were responsible for abuses of power and crimes against their holy orders. With Parliament supporting the King by choice, Henry was able to present himself as doing the right thing for his country, not merely suiting his own needs. Henry rewarded Cromwell handsomely for his troubles, giving him various titles and offices, including Chancellor of the Exchequer after Thomas More resigned from the post.

With the King's marriage to Anne now formalized, Cromwell aided him in weakening the Church in order to discredit the institution more easily. The Submission of the Clergy was followed by the Act of Succession, both of which gave more power to the King. This led to More and Fisher, who both refused to swear to the oath, being executed for treason. Slowly but surely, Cromwell was removing other powerful men from the King's council. It was Cromwell's revisions that made it an act of treason to speak out against the King or royal family.

Next appointed vicegerent in 1535, Cromwell now had power over the Church. He undertook the *Valor Ecclesiasticus* in order to determine the wealth of the

Below: Forced to endure the insult of defending the legality of her marriage, Catherine of Aragon is shown here during the inquiry called by Henry. Catherine always called herself the King's "true and legitimate wife," but the inquiry ended in divorce.

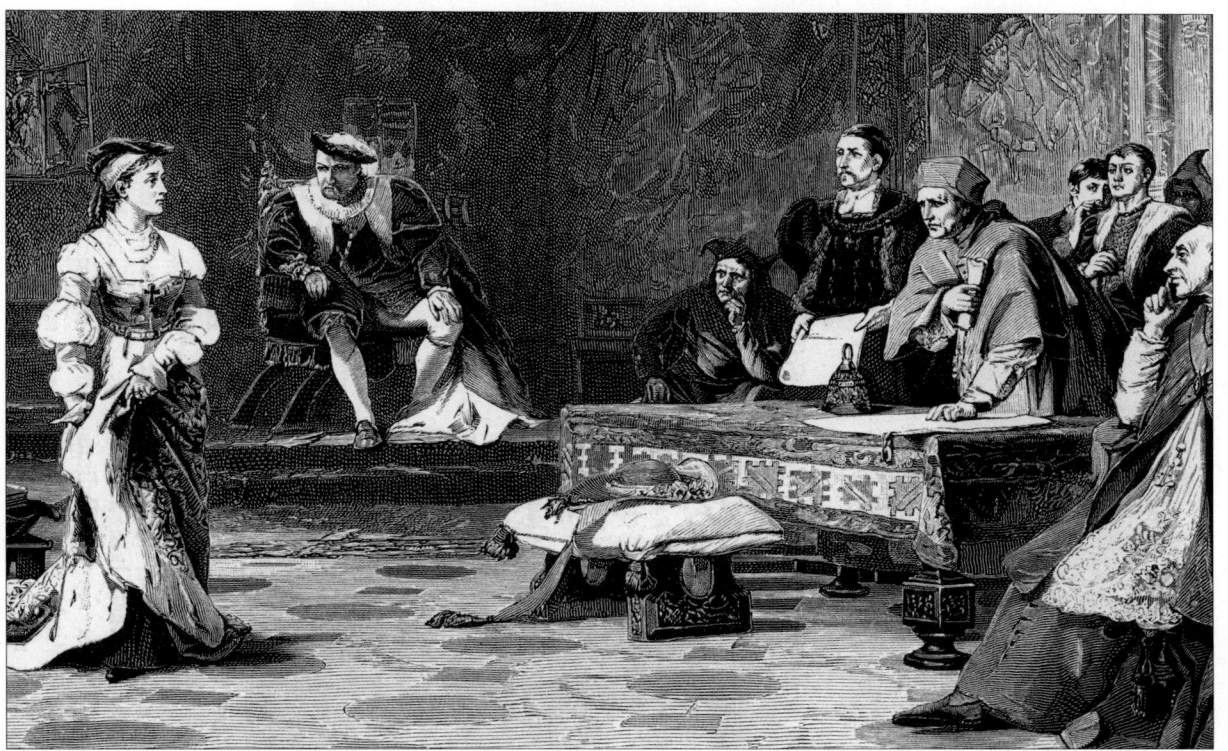

Left: Thomas Cromwell is shown here painted by Hans Holbein the Younger (ca. 1532–1533). After demanding Cromwell's execution, Henry blamed Cromwell's enemies for misleading him.

including her brother, George—leading to their executions. This also allowed him to remove Thomas Boleyn, Anne's father, from his position as Lord Privy Seal, which Cromwell took on July 2, 1536. Just a week later, Cromwell was made Baron of Wimbledon. It seemed that his influence over Henry had been cemented and that he could do no wrong in Henry's eyes. But his power had made him careless. The cold eyes of the King were upon him and past experience had taught Cromwell that falling from favor never ended well.

Henry's actions towards the men and women loyal to him show us a King who would stop at nothing to get his own way. He could be ruthless, cruel and detached, discarding anyone who did not agree with him without a second thought. Yet Henry truly seemed to believe he was right in his actions and that what was good for the King was good for the entire country. In terms of ditching anyone he tired of, Henry VIII was only just getting started.

clergy in England. This led to the Suppression of the Lesser Monasteries in 1536. Anne Boleyn, once a supporter of Cromwell's as he aided her marriage to Henry, turned against Cromwell as she felt that this money should be used for charity. Her chaplains spoke openly against him and were supported by his other enemies.

But Cromwell was about to prove his immense power. Anne had not yet produced a male heir and her hold over the King was weakening. Cromwell used this, plus her flirtatious nature, to his advantage and started gathering evidence of Anne's infidelity. He was part of the court that tried Anne and her supposed lovers—

Opposite: This woodcut print was made for the coronation of Anne Boleyn on June 1, 1533. The illustration shows Anne and Henry in a happy, affectionate pose. Just under three years later, she was executed for incest, adultery and high treason.

The noble tryum=

phaunt coronacyon of quene Anne/
wyfe vnto the moost noble kynge
Henry the. viij.

HENRY VIII: MATCHING, HATCHING AND DISPATCHING

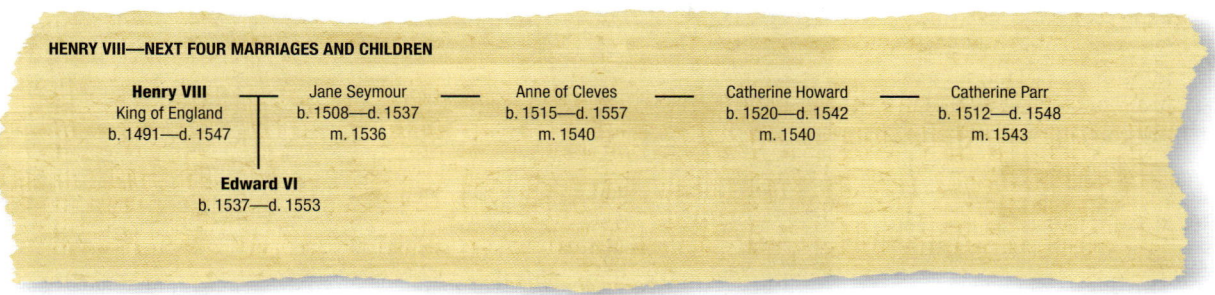

HENRY VIII—NEXT FOUR MARRIAGES AND CHILDREN

| **Henry VIII**
King of England
b. 1491—d. 1547 | **Jane Seymour**
b. 1508—d. 1537
m. 1536 | **Anne of Cleves**
b. 1515—d. 1557
m. 1540 | **Catherine Howard**
b. 1520—d. 1542
m. 1540 | **Catherine Parr**
b. 1512—d. 1548
m. 1543 |

Edward VI
b. 1537—d. 1553

As the rumblings of religious discontent grew, Henry VIII discarded his closest advisors one by one, treating his Queens with the same contempt. Showing no concern for his subjects' wealth, occupation or religion, the King's arrogance knew no bounds. Henry had always liked things done his way. Now Supreme Head of the Church of England as well as King, Henry saw himself as invulnerable. With the blood of several loyal men already on his hands, it was time to show everyone that Henry's word was God's will and the law of the land.

Divorced, beheaded, died;
Divorced, beheaded, survived.

It was in 1536 that the powder keg of discontent Henry had stirred up exploded. From reducing the power of the Church and bestowing it upon himself to destroying and pillaging much-loved monasteries,

Opposite: This illustration of the Pilgrimage of Grace shows church figures proudly bearing religious icons as they protest against the tide of reform. Henry VIII may have been a force to be reckoned with, but these pilgrims and many others were prepared to die for their faith.

Henry seemed to be unstoppable. The public still suffered from enforced loans for foreign battles to appease Henry's appetite for war and now they were losing their religious heritage, having to bear the agony of watching churches destroyed and their beloved monks and nuns being turned out with nowhere to go. Enough was enough.

Beginning of the Backlash
The first mass revolt occurred in Lincolnshire, just days before the more problematic Pilgrimage of Grace. Desperate at the treatment of the monks of Louth Abbey and in fear of the confiscation of their holy

THE DUKE OF NORFOLK

THOMAS HOWARD (pictured right), a politician, was a member of Henry's council who enjoyed the King's favor on Wolsey's downfall (the two were opposed in their ideas on war). Howard was Anne Boleyn's uncle and eager to aid Henry's divorce to Catherine so that Henry would be free to marry Anne. Howard benefitted from this alliance and made sure he stayed loyal to the King, to the point of turning against Anne when she stood trial for treason. Devious and duplicitous, Howard took advantage of the downfall of others to climb the greasy pole of power, helping to bring down Cromwell, among others.

He was also Catherine Howard's uncle and instrumental in their marriage. It was only when Catherine's adultery became public knowledge that Howard began his fall from grace. Despite him desperately trying to win back favor, Howard and his son, Henry, were arrested in 1547 for treason, with his entire family standing against him. Henry was executed and Howard only escaped execution due to Henry VIII's convenient death. A conservative Catholic, he was restored to his Dukedom under Queen Mary in 1553.

relics, a large force of protestors, numbering in the tens of thousands, marched to Lincoln Cathedral, led by a priest and a shoemaker nicknamed "Captain Cobbler." Their demands were simple. The people wanted freedom to worship as they always had done.

Henry met the revolt with a wave of violence. Charles Brandon, Mary Tudor's husband and the Duke of Suffolk, was sent to disperse the crowds and the main ringleaders were swiftly executed. After seeing this, the rest of the protestors speedily fled for home. How far this early uprising led to the Pilgrimage of Grace is disputed, but the harsh treatment of the crowds in Lincolnshire certainly angered the rest of the country. Nobles and commoners alike banded together to fight back against the tyrannical monarch.

> … the only source of extra food and financial alms during these straitened times, the monasteries were often a real necessity.

The chief complaint was the treatment of the churches and religious houses. For many communities, the church was the focal point of their lives and Henry's changes were too much, too soon, for a way of life that had been shared over many generations. Henry's treatment of Catherine had also angered the public, but so too had his cruel dispatch of Anne, the woman for whom he had brought about these changes. Had Henry no idea that he was asking his people to renounce some of the practices that were traditionally thought to get people into heaven? Or did the tyrannical King just not care for his subjects' souls in his never-ending quest for satisfaction? (A secondary objective of the revolt was to reinstate Princess Mary as successor to the throne, her Catholic sympathies being well known.)

Pilgrimage of Grace: For God and the King

The insurgent pilgrims, led by the barrister Robert Aske, travelled through Beverley and Hull before occupying the walled town of York where they reinstated the monks and nuns and restored the Catholic observances that Henry had deemed unlawful. With the smaller monasteries being the only source of extra food and financial alms during these straitened times, the monasteries were often a real necessity. This was a rebellion on a much larger scale than in Lincoln. Henry and his men knew they would have to tread a little more carefully. The Duke of Norfolk, with the Earl of Shrewsbury leading the King's army, was sent to converse with Aske and the ringleaders, with the assurance that Henry would listen to their demands. A resulting promise of a general pardon and Parliament being convened to discuss the concerns meant that the naive rebels disbanded, believing that they had made progress and their case to uphold the values of the Church would be heard. It is thought that Aske and his followers were of the opinion that the King had been misadvised and did not fully understand the reality of the reforms. Although Henry was initially angry with Norfolk for acquiescing to the rebels, the rebels had been dispersed and he now had time on his side to deal with the disturbance.

Yet Henry had no intention of backing down or stopping the dissolution. Meeting with Aske himself, Henry fed him platitudes and blamed Cromwell for much of the reformation. When another rebellion broke out in 1537, Henry took this as the rebels not keeping their word, even though it was widely known that this new uprising was nothing to do with Aske or his followers. Henry had Aske seized along with other prominent ringleaders and the men were quickly executed. The aggrieved King had a point to prove and over 220 people were put to death for their defiance, with many of their corpses prominently displayed to warn others. Henry showed no compassion, executing nobles, priests, monks and commoners alike and even making family members sit in on the trials, such as they were. Such a large-scale removal of the leaders was successful and the uprising was quelled. Everyone knew that Henry was literally taking no prisoners.

> The aggrieved King had a point to prove and over 220 people were put to death for their defiance, with many of their corpses prominently displayed to warn others.

… the spirited character that Henry had so admired before they were married did not seem so attractive now that she was Queen.

In the end, the pilgrims were unable to end the dissolution of the monasteries or the desecration of relics and shrines. However, while the pilgrims were crushed, public support for their cause and the traditional Church remained and would cause turmoil for later Tudor monarchs.

The New Queen

With Anne already pregnant, the early signs for this second marriage were promising. Anne was not a great beauty but was sexy, intelligent and certainly knew how to work her assets (Henry was thought to be especially fond of her figure). Now carrying Henry's child, it seemed as if the future of the Tudor monarchy was once again secure. On September 7, 1533, Anne gave birth to Elizabeth, who would one day rule England herself. As the 1533 Act of Succession had made Mary—Henry's daughter by Catherine—illegitimate, Elizabeth was now heir to the throne of England. Anne had quickly proven that she could bear healthy children, but Henry still did not have the son and heir he had dreamed of. Also, his new bride was proving to be a handful. Forthright and tactical, the spirited character that Henry had so admired before they were married did not seem so attractive now that she was Queen.

Always an arrogant woman, believing herself to be everything Henry could ever want, Anne paid no heed to the callous way Henry had dispatched Catherine from his life. Her lifestyle and court was even grander that Catherine's. The exacting Queen had over 60 personal ladies-in-waiting and hundreds of servants to attend to her every whim. During their courtship, Henry had showered Anne with gifts and she felt that she had been born for this extravagant lifestyle. Henry even made Anne a peer, making her the Marquess of Pembroke in 1532. Yet her imperious nature and sharp tongue would not earn Anne any loyalty among her servants or her equals.

Her cause was not helped by the fact that Anne had two miscarriages in quick succession. She fell pregnant

Above: Anne's letter to Cardinal Wolsey thanking him for supporting her marriage to the king. Ever the politician, Anne writes that she is in Wolsey's debt, which she will repay when in a position of power.

again in 1535 and the couple hoped for the best. However, fate was about to turn against her. Catherine of Aragon died on January 8, 1536. Anne and Henry celebrated, united again in their joy. But theirs was a fleeting happiness. On January 29, the same day of Catherine's funeral, Anne miscarried a male child. She put it down to stress caused by Henry's fall during a jousting match, but in Henry's eyes only Anne was to

Opposite: There are many rumors about Anne Boleyn's appearance, including her having warts, double chins and the infamous sixth finger! However, this portrait shows us an attractive woman with the striking eyes and "pretty ducks" (breasts) that Henry was so fond of.

Above: Anne Boleyn swoons following the news that she has been condemned to death in this painting by French artist Pierre-Nolasque Bergeret, circa 1814.

blame. Henry had truly loved his second wife and had feelings for her still, but now felt sure that he would never have a son with Anne and began to plot her removal by any means necessary.

Not letting his true feelings be known to his wife, who may still bear him an heir, Henry discussed his situation with his trusted advisors, turning to Cromwell for a solution. Anne had made herself many powerful enemies during her short time as Queen, including Charles Brandon, the Duke of Suffolk and her uncle, Thomas Howard, the Duke of Norfolk, who had earlier supported the union. There were very few people willing to go out on a limb to support the new Queen. With one troublesome divorce already behind him,

Henry was correct in thinking that a second would be much harder to explain away. He was also sure that Anne would not bear the insult quietly. There had to be another way to get rid of Anne while keeping public support with the King.

The Case Against the Queen

Anne's strong willed, flirtatious nature, which Henry had once found so beguiling, now contributed to her downfall. Led by Cromwell's machinations, two separate accounts came to light of Anne being unfaithful to Henry. The first, Sir Henry Norris, refused to admit to these claims, but Mark Smeaton,

Opposite: Anne's short marriage ended at Tower Green, where she was executed by sword; a quicker and more merciful death than the axe. The executioner wields the heavy sword with two hands, which generally meant that a single stroke was enough to sever the neck.

EXECUTIONS, TUDOR STYLE

TOWER HILL WAS the official execution site of the Tower during its time as a prison. The accused were taken from their cells up to the site on Tower Hill, where they were met with the block and an executioner armed with an axe. It was also likely that they would have to pass through the jeering crowds who had gathered to watch their death. Executioners were not paid for their work by the crown. Instead, they depended on tips from the prisoners. The amount they were paid could result in a far quicker death, depending on how sympathetic or experienced the axe-wielder was. Noblewomen, such as Anne Boleyn, Catherine Howard and Lady Jane Grey, were executed on Tower Green, away from the common criminals.

TO COMMEMORATE THE TRAGIC HISTORY AND
IN MANY CASES THE MARTYRDOM OF THOSE
WHO FOR THE SAKE OF THEIR FAITH COUNTRY
OR IDEALS STAKED THEIR LIVES AND LOST

ON THIS SITE MORE THAN 125 WERE PUT TO DEATH
THE NAMES OF SOME OF WHOM ARE RECORDED HERE

Above: This plaque forms part of the poignant memorial at Tower Hill, which marks the spot of those who died there. Many were executed under Henry VIII, including Fisher, More and Cromwell.

Opposite: Jane Seymour, pictured here, looks sweet and demure but it is rumored that she flaunted a locket from Henry in front of Anne, who received a similar piece when Henry courted her.

a court musician and music teacher, admitted to having an affair with Anne after she seduced him. It is possible that he was tortured into his confession (an ordeal that Norris, as a nobleman, would have been spared), however he did repeat its truth on his execution for treason, perhaps knowing that he was doomed to death. But the case against Anne did not end there. In total, five men were executed for having dallied with the Queen, including George Boleyn, Anne's own brother. Three more were accused but escaped death.

It was now Anne's turn to face a trial. The ridiculous nature of many of the claims has shown just how determined Henry was for her to die. Any affection he might once have held for his wife and the mother of his child had died and Henry was eager to move on, having already chosen a replacement for Anne. Claims that she had used witchcraft to seduce the King and other lovers were rife and she was hit with claims of adultery, incest and witchcraft before being charged with high treason and taken to the Tower. There were even rumors of her having poisoned Catherine of Aragon and plotting to kill Henry's children by other women. The nail in her coffin was a charge (with no supportable evidence) of plotting with her lovers to kill the King in order to marry Henry Norris. Henry VIII was clearly leaving nothing to chance.

Right: Just as with his marriage to Catherine, Henry needed a dispensation to marry Jane, the likely reason she was distantly relation of one of his previous wives.

On May 14, Thomas Cranmer, earlier one of Anne's supporters, declared their marriage to be dissolved. Five days later Anne was executed on Tower Green. Declaring her absolute innocence to the last, Anne blessed her faithless husband and asked God to have mercy on her maligned soul. She escaped the horrific death of burning, which was often administered to women accused of treason, and instead was swiftly dispatched by a sword. Still protesting her innocence and love for Henry, her "little neck" was no match for the sharp blade. The rumors of witchcraft were given weight when the executioner lifted high her disembodied head, the eyes and lips moved in death.

While many of the allegations against Anne seem spurious, the sheer number of men involved in her life means that Anne is often viewed as a promiscuous whore. Whatever the truth, her wretched death and the reasons given for it were certainly convenient for Henry. Although this marriage caused the split from

> This reunion was no easy task, as Henry had viciously disowned Mary. She naturally supported her mother and was sent away from court after their divorce.

the Catholic Church and did not result in a long love or the desired male heir, its consequence was one of England's most famous and influential monarchs— Elizabeth I.

Third Time's the Charm

After his tormented and unsatisfying marriage to Anne, Henry stayed well away from anyone intelligent and forthright. He had learned his lesson. Jane Seymour had been one of the court's ladies-in-waiting, serving both Catherine and Anne before their elimination. Henry had long found Jane attractive. He admired her gentle ways and modest, charming attitude; a stark comparison to the seductive Anne and the obstinate Catherine. Jane was also not very educated or political, preferring to involve herself in domestic issues rather than man's work. It seemed that in Jane, Henry would finally have the ideal wife, someone more like his adored mother.

Opposite: Jane Seymour was the only one of Henry's wives to give him what he wanted most, a son and heir. Edward is pictured here as the Prince of Wales, a title he was given just a week after his birth. Even though he is not yet King, Edward looks every inch the monarch.

The couple were engaged on May 20, 1536, the very day after Anne's execution, and were married just ten days later. Jane strove to reunite Henry with his daughter Mary after he had classed her as illegitimate following the breakup with Catherine of Aragon. While the line of succession was not yet restored, Jane did manage to reconcile the two somewhat and she became known for her compassion. This reunion was no easy task, as Henry had viciously disowned Mary. She naturally supported her mother and was sent away from court after their divorce.

On October 12, 1537, Jane gave the King the son and heir he had longed for. Christened Edward, the boy's birth was cause for much celebration and joy. Henry finally had his "great matter." Yet the joy was curtailed soon after, for on October 24, Jane succumbed to the infection—possibly puerperal fever—that had followed her difficult labour and died. Henry was truly saddened by her death. Perhaps because she did not argue with him, perhaps because she gave him a son and perhaps because he really did love her, Jane is thought to be Henry's favorite wife. He ordered 12,000 masses to be said for her soul, wore black for three months and, although he and his advisors soon began the search for a new wife, did not marry again for three years.

Jane was the only one of Henry's wives to receive a Queen's funeral and on his death they were buried together at Windsor Castle, which he himself requested in his will. It is said that some of Henry's last words were of Jane, the only wife to give him what he needed. However, if she had lived, who knows what fate might have awaited her from her fickle husband?

The King's Beloved Sister

Eager for Henry to make a politically advantageous

TUDOR HEALTH AND CHILDBIRTH

STAYING HEALTHY IN Tudor times was always a gamble, no matter who you were. Diet, hygiene and lifestyle were unhealthy and there was little or no idea about how infections were spread. Jane's death from a complication of childbirth was a common event, as were deaths in childhood from tuberculosis, consumption and sweating sickness. On average, people died much younger than they do today, with the average age being around 35–40 years old. There was an outbreak of bubonic plague in 1535, brought about by infected fleas on rats. Such epidemics were made worse by lack of sewage systems and poor sanitation.

marriage with his next wife now that he had sired at least one son, Cromwell and his advisors suggested Anne of Cleves. With alliances with France and Spain ever shifting and Francis I of France and Charles V having recently signed a peace treaty, forming an alliance with Germany was seen as a sensible move. The Duke of Cleves, Anne's brother, was a potential ally against the threat of Rome and the might of the Catholic Church should they choose to contest Henry's violent treatment of the monasteries. Hans Holbein painted both Anne and her sister, Amalia, as the next potential wife of Henry and Queen of England. While his portrait of Anne is thought to be overly flattering, many see it as realistic, showing her to be sweet-looking and attractive. Much was made of her charm and modesty, but she was unsophisticated, spoke almost no English and had no skills in music, dancing or other courtly attributes.

However, on the basis of the portrait and advice of his council, Henry sent Cromwell to arrange

the marriage treaty, which was finalized in October 1539, despite the betrothed couple never having met in person. Anne duly made the long sea journey to England. Her first experience with her husband-to-be

Right: Describing his fourth wife, Anne of Cleves, Henry was heard to say "I like her not" and used her appearance as the reason for not consummating their marriage!

was unsettling, to say the least. Henry, with several of his friends, entered her room dressed in masks and cloaks. Henry then leapt on his unsuspecting fiancée, embracing and kissing her. Anne did not react well to the joke, allegedly shouting for help and cursing the men, having no idea this was her husband-to-be. From then on, Henry was ill-disposed to go through with the marriage, saying that Anne was not as attractive as her portrait and had no sense of humor. He is thought to have dubbed her the "Flanders mare." Despite Henry's misgivings, the couple were wed on January 6, 1540. It is likely that his advisors, Cromwell especially, stressed the usefulness of a German alliance to ensure the union. They also played on Henry's fears of securing a Tudor succession by the provision of a "spare."

But the marriage was a disaster. Neither party wanted to consummate it and it was only a matter of months before Henry pressed for an annulment on these grounds.

Here, Anne could have proved most difficult, despite their lack of sex life being common knowledge among their companions, who feared there would never be another heir. But Anne, eager herself to avoid a physical relationship with her husband and not wanting to end up like her predecessor Anne Boleyn, gratefully jumped at the annulment. Henry was so thankful to be easily rid of her without offending her family that he awarded Anne money and properties. After the annulment, Anne was often invited to court and the two remained friends. Anne even became known as the King's "beloved" or "good sister." She never remarried, having sufficient funds to live well for the rest of her life.

As Anne had little family left in Germany, she remained in England for the rest of her life, surrounding herself with female courtiers and living in

Above: To the satisfaction of both parties—especially Anne, who kept her head—Henry's brief marriage to Anne was annulled only six months after they were wed. This is the official nullification of the union.

THE CAPRICIOUS KING

AFTER CROMWELL'S DEATH, Henry soon felt he had acted rashly. Now remembering all that Cromwell had done for him, Henry came to regret his decision and eventually blamed it on his advisors.

Cromwell had certainly proved his loyalty and constantly acted in the interests of his King and country. His own personal views on reformation, plus political maneuvrings and the blame placed at his feet for Henry's marriage to Anne of Cleves, were what led to his death, but Cromwell was truly the King's man. Henry's mercurial nature led the King to later regret the beheading of a loyal, faithful man, a character trait that reoccurs throughout his reign with men and women suffering for falling out of his favor.

> Continuing with the dissolution of the monasteries at least brought Henry money, but Cromwell's actions against the idolatry of the Church were a step too far in Henry's largely orthodox eyes.

peace. She outlived Henry and all his wives, dying in 1557. Anne is buried in Westminster Abbey, the only one of Henry's wives to be laid there. It could be said that she was the luckiest of his wives and shows how appreciative he could be to those who submitted to his will.

Another One Bites the Dust

While Anne's marriage ended well for her, it brought about the downfall of one of Henry VIII's most infamous advisors. Never happy giving anyone else too much power, especially if it meant relinquishing it himself, Henry had been willing to use Cromwell's forceful political skills and sharp intelligence up to a point. But Cromwell was now taking the reformation too far, suggesting changes to the Church that Henry was not happy to make. Continuing with the dissolution of the monasteries at least brought Henry money, but Cromwell's actions against the idolatry of the Church were a step too far in Henry's largely orthodox eyes. The more conservative branch of the Church who supported Henry in this started to move against Cromwell, but he worked quickly to suppress them, using his own revisions to the Act of Supremacy to execute several potentially powerful men for treason. A backlash to the reformation had started, but Cromwell had gone too far to stop now. Henry was actually quite a traditional Catholic and felt that Cromwell was approaching heresy in his actions towards the Church. It was this, plus his part in Henry's marriage to Anne of Cleves, that led to Cromwell's downfall.

Henry was truly furious at feeling he had been coerced into marriage to Anne of Cleves. Fearing another long, drawn-out divorce, his anger made him turn to some of Cromwell's enemies, most notably the Duke of Norfolk, who called Cromwell a traitor and organized his arrest. Eager to defeat Cromwell, a list of offenses was drawn up, becoming the Bill of Attainder by which Cromwell was sentenced to death without trial or a single supporter. This bill included treason and heresy. Cromwell was also accused of plotting to marry Mary Tudor and supplant Henry on the throne, finding that his enemies were all too eager to support any allegations Henry might charge him with. Henry felt that Cromwell had gone too far. He also knew that Francis I, who Henry was eager to curry favor with, despised Cromwell. The faithful advisor had outlived his use and it was time for him to go.

Cromwell is often portrayed as a harsh, villainous man, but he did leave behind a legacy that still shaped Britain. He was a leading hand in the writing of the Great Bible, first released in English in 1539.

Opposite: This image of the Great Bible gives us a glimpse of what would have been in most churches in England by the mid-sixteenth century. The frontispiece directs clergy to place it where all could read it.

DIEV ET MON DROIT

GREENSLEEVES

HENRY VIII WAS FOND of music and he was a talented musician. He loved the idea of the Renaissance court, filled with skilled performers and learned men who could discuss theology, art and philosophy. Henry's own skill with music is well known, he could play many instruments and could write music and poetry. Henry wrote *Pastimes with Good Company* (known as the *Kynge's Ballade*). It was also widely speculated that he wrote the popular *Greensleeves* (see below), but this was never proven and is now thought to be unlikely.

Setting up various bureaucratic institutions, Cromwell brought order and stability to much of England and ensured that the vast amount of money he earned the King was put to good use, including starting the legislation for poor relief in 1536. He was largely responsible for turning a medieval form of government into a more modern version, with separate departments—each receiving a certain amount of money and being run by a group of people—so that no one person held all the power. Cromwell also supported commoners—or whoever the most able person was—in these roles, as opposed to nobles who may have had their own agenda.

Opposite: Henry VIII is pictured here in an elaborate, ornate portrait. The powerful King looks stern and alarming, although he is starting to show signs of aging. He is posed in front of the motto of an English monarch. Particularly fitting for Henry VIII, it reads "God and my right."

Moving on With Haste
Another childless marriage behind him, Henry was beginning to worry about his lack of legitimate children. Despite being 49 and very overweight, he still had an eye for the ladies. With past experience of political alliances never turning out well (wives one, two and four attesting to this fact), Henry decided to

turn to his wife's ladies-in-waiting for his fifth wife. He married Catherine Howard (the niece of the Duke of Norfolk) on July 28, 1540, the very day of Cromwell's execution. Having long admired Catherine, who at just 19 was 32 years younger than her husband, Catherine's sparkling youth and vivacity were very attractive to Henry. Equally, the dazzling and expensive gifts he showered on Catherine were attractive to the bubbly girl. At first, the two reveled in their passionate marriage. Henry enjoyed his sexy young bride, believing that she would easily bear his children. Her family were well rewarded too, gaining a reputation for taking advantage of Henry's happiness and securing positions and wealth for themselves.

> Seeming to lack any self-control or self-preservation instincts, she took up with Thomas Culpepper, a courtier whom she had been attracted to before Henry decided to marry her.

The Young Seductress

The honeymoon period would soon be over as Catherine's youthful exploits would return to haunt her. After the death of her parents, Catherine had spent time in the household of her step-grandmother, the Dowager Duchess of Norfolk. The Duchess spent little time at home and left her young ward to take care of herself. It was in this household that Catherine met Henry Mannox, a music teacher with whom she engaged in a sexual relationship. A few years later, now

> … now no stranger to the arts of lovemaking, Catherine fell for Francis Dereham, the secretary of the Duchess' household.

no stranger to the arts of lovemaking, Catherine fell for Francis Dereham, the secretary of the Duchess' household. They also became lovers and in fact may have planned to marry. However, when the Duchess found out about their relationship, Catherine was sent to court to wait on Anne of Cleves.

If her youthful indiscretions had ended there, perhaps little harm would have been done. But Catherine's lust could not be sated by an old King past his prime. Seeming to lack any self-control or self-preservation instincts, she took up with Thomas Culpepper, a courtier whom she had been attracted to before Henry decided to marry her. Catherine and Henry had not been married for a year when she started her affair with Culpepper. It was at this stage that things began to unravel for the imprudent and thoughtless Queen. Used to getting her own way with men, Catherine was aghast when Francis Dereham reappeared. Dereham was appointed as Catherine's personal secretary, possibly to buy his silence, a decision that would lead to both their downfall.

Henry was informed about her indiscretions. First refusing to believe them, he sent Cranmer to confront

Opposite: This portrait of Catherine Howard does not belie the girlish coquetry that Henry found so attractive in his fifth wife. Here the expensively dressed Catherine looks more like Jane Seymour or Anne of Cleves than Anne Boleyn, yet she was to share Anne's grisly fate.

ENGLISH NAVAL POWER

While the English Navy was largely established under Henry VII, it did not become such a widely used and pioneering force until the reign of Elizabeth I. However, Henry VIII developed the navy by building larger ships with more guns. England now also kept an active defensive navy during peacetime. The *Mary Rose* sunk in the Battle of the Solent, the result of France unsuccessfully invading England after the battles in 1544. Salvaged in 1982, the Mary Rose is now a museum ship.

Catherine Howard.

Left: Probably written in 1541, one year after her marriage to Henry, this is a love letter from Catherine Howard to her lover, Thomas Culpeper. Catherine writes: "It makes my heart die to think I cannot be always in your company." Her words would soon ring true.

her and demand the truth. If Catherine had been honest and told of the understanding between herself and Dereham to be married, her life might have been spared even if her marriage was finished. But she lied, saying that Dereham had forced himself on her. Dereham denied any relationship between them after Catherine's marriage, instead placing this blame on Culpeper, knowing that Catherine had found him attractive.

As the evidence against her was mounting, it was when Culpeper confessed that he and the Queen had planned to start an affair that Catherine no longer had a chance of survival. A letter from Catherine was also found, which stated that she longed to see and speak with him. Devastated, with his pride in tatters, Henry lashed out. Both Dereham and Culpeper were executed for treason (Culpeper only being spared the trial of hanged, drawn and quartered as he was a previous favorite of the King).

Catherine was taken to the Tower through Traitor's gate on February 10, 1542. On a chilling note, the boat that carried her passed right beneath the heads of Culpeper and Dereham, whose sentences had already been carried out. Catherine was held in the Tower for three short days until her execution on February 13 on Tower Green. Aged 21 when she died, she was one of the youngest women to be executed, only beaten by Lady Jane Grey in 1554 (whose exact date of birth is unknown).

> Catherine was taken to the Tower … On a chilling note, the boat that carried her passed right beneath the heads of Culpeper and Dereham, whose sentences had already been carried out.

Above: Catherine Howard is here being conveyed down the River Thames on her journey to the Tower of London. While her attendants weep for her, Catherine herself appears to be in a state of shock.

The Survivor

Henry married for the sixth and final time on July 12, 1543. His sixth wife was Catherine Parr, a 31-year-old woman who had been married twice before. Here Henry had a wife who was not too young or oversexed, too cunning or flirtatious, too maidenly or frigid, or too uneducated or silly. With Catherine, perhaps Henry would find happiness.

It is widely thought that Catherine acted largely as Henry's nursemaid during their married life. However, although she would have tried to improve and lighten his mood, it is unlikely that she would actually have

Above: This illustration shows Henry's sixth wedding to Catherine Parr, who would outlive him. Catherine was enamored with Thomas Seymour—Jane Seymour's brother—when Henry made his feelings for her known. Thomas was removed from the court shortly after.

THOMAS SEYMOUR

THOMAS AND EDWARD were the brothers of Jane Seymour. They used their sister's marriage to further their own power and status within the royal court. A power-hungry schemer, Thomas went as far as planning to marry Princess Elizabeth after Catherine Parr's death to become King himself. Even when married to Catherine, Thomas would bestow an alarming amount of attention on the young teenaged princess, who was still under her stepmother's care. In fact, Catherine even found the two of them locked in an embrace once, leading to Elizabeth's removal from the household.

> This led to his displeasure and, in 1546, her Catholic enemies even drew up an arrest warrant for her on the King's behalf ...

nursed him physically. Henry would have had a vast team of physicians to take care of his health. What is true is that Catherine was a devoted, caring and loving wife. Their marriage was at times tumultuous. Catherine had reformist, even Protestant, leanings and she would often argue with Henry about religion.

This led to his displeasure and, in 1546, her Catholic enemies even drew up an arrest warrant for her on the King's behalf, but she found out about the charges against her. Going straight to the King, Catherine won him round, saying that many of her arguments were designed to frustrate him, thereby taking his mind off the painful ulcer on his leg. She also flattered his ego by telling Henry she learned from his responses.

The pair were reunited and thought to be fond of one another until Henry's death. Henry may not have loved his sixth wife with the ardent passion he felt for some of his past wives, but they were friends and he could trust and depend on Catherine. Certainly Henry took pains to support her after his death, leaving her a generous allowance.

Catherine was also trusted enough to be given the title of Regent when Henry was fighting in France in 1544 (only to be deceived by Charles V, who

Below: Here we see Henry VIII with his Privy Council. Eager to ensure that the throne of his son, Edward, would be safe from usurpation after his death, Henry's will stated that sixteen councillors would advise Edward, not giving any single man the chance to snatch power.

HANS HOLBEIN THE YOUNGER

HOLBEIN IS A German artist widely accepted to be the best portrait painter of the sixteenth century. The official King's Painter from 1535, his paintings looking like a *Who's Who* of Tudor court. His precise style and intricate eye for detail is mixed with layers of symbolism and allegory, with his famous portrait of Henry VIII being a prime example. The realism with which he painted people means that we can largely rely on his portraits to glimpse long-dead people (although his portrait of Anne of Cleves was famously flattering).

Opposite: Unlucky in love: This nineteenth-century print shows Henry VIII surrounded by portraits of each of his six wives. In clockwise order from the top are: Anne of Cleves; Catherine Howard; Anne Boleyn; Catherine of Aragon; Catherine Parr; and Jane Seymour.

Above: This self portrait of Hans Holbein the Younger shows the detail and realism in his paintings. He also experimented with anamorphism in "The Ambassadors" (1533), in which a distorted skull can be seen perfectly when viewed from the extreme right of the painting.

negotiated a separate peace with Francis I). Her uncle, Thomas Cranmer, saw to it that the Queen Regent was supported, but it was her own loyalty and strength of character that saw her successfully manage the French campaign from home while protecting the country from any potential threat from Scotland.

Catherine worked hard to finally reunite Henry with his estranged daughters. The Third Act of Succession in 1543 restored Mary and Elizabeth to the line of succession behind Edward and any of his children, provided that his daughters married with the council's consent. It was this Act that would later put a swift end to Lady Jane Grey's rule after Edward VI.

On Henry's death, Catherine quickly remarried, having to do so in secret as it was not seemly for a Queen Dowager to take a new husband so soon after the King's death. Thomas Seymour, an old flame of Catherine's, became her fourth husband (she is known as the English Queen who was married the most). This marriage also had its ups and downs. Seymour had previously tried to marry Elizabeth, Catherine's step-daughter, before settling for Catherine herself.

Catherine later gave birth to her only child, Mary, on August 30, 1548. She died shortly afterwards from puerperal fever, the same infection that killed Jane Seymour.

The fact that she and Henry had no children is perhaps down to Henry's failing health at the time of their marriage. Now in his mid 50s, with a turbulent and voracious life behind him, Henry was hugely obese. Far from the active, sporting young man he used to be, the aged King now needed help to move around. This excessive diet and lack of exercise may have been the cause of many of his health problems, which included gout, skin complaints and possible diabetes. He suffered from a bad fall during a jousting

Above: Nearing the end of his life, bloated and in constant pain, Henry VIII found it hard even to walk by his mid-50s. Neither his wife, nor any of his children were with him when he died. Pictured here, Henry is a sobering reminder that not even great kings live forever.

a bloody sea of executions, reformation and violence. Fading away—the exact cause of his death is unknown—Henry died in the presence of Archbishop Cranmer, one of the few advisors close to the King to avoid execution, and perhaps the closest person Henry had to a true friend.

Many versions of Henry VIII's final words exist, including him calling out for Jane Seymour, his favorite wife who had given him the son he so dearly wanted. Other versions have him raving "Monks, monks, monks!" perhaps never being able to forgive himself for his crimes against the faithful servants of his Church. In reality, the aged King would have found it difficult to speak at all. As always, the great equalizer of death proved to be even more powerful than this most magnificent and formidable of Kings.

Henry was a man of great personality and determination who lived his life to the full, never allowing potential consequences to impede his search for happiness and fulfillment. The King was able to inspire men to follow him, even if he did not always think through the consequences of where he was leading them. The supremacy he took as his birthright meant that no one could challenge his actions. If remembered for nothing else, Henry VIII was a true and mighty King in the eyes of his subjects and remains a source of fascination to this very day.

match in 1536 (which was the possible cause of Anne Boleyn's miscarriage of a son). The wound had festered for years and often reopened, causing pain and much discomfort. It also further curtailed any activity, including his sex life.

Henry VIII died at the age of 55, the fun and frivolity of his magnificent early court forgotten in

Opposite: Henry VIII is buried in St. George's Chapel in Windsor Castle. His remains lie beneath this marble memorial plaque in a vault he shares with Jane Seymour. Over a hundred years later, King Charles I was interred into the same vault.

IN A VAULT
BENEATH THIS MARBLE SLAB
ARE DEPOSITED THE REMAINS
OF
JANE SEYMOUR QUEEN OF KING HENRY VIII
- 1537 -
KING HENRY VIII.
- 1547. -
KING CHARLES I.
- 1648. -
AND
AN INFANT CHILD OF QUEEN ANNE.

THIS MEMORIAL WAS PLACED HERE
BY COMMAND OF
KING WILLIAM IV. 1837.

PARVVLE PATRISSA, PATRIÆ VIRTVTIS ET HÆRES
ESTO, NIHIL MAIVS MAXIMVS ORBIS HABET.
GNATVM VIX POSSVNT COELVM ET NATVRA DEDISSE,
HVIVS QVEM PATRIS, VICTVS HONORET HONOS.
ÆQVATO TANTVM, TANTI TV FACTA PARENTIS,
VOTA HOMINVM, VIX QVO PROGREDIANTVR, HABENT
VINCITO, VICISTI. QVOT REGES PRISCVS ADORAT
ORBIS NEC TE QVI VINCERE POSSIT ERIT.

EDWARD VI: REFORMS, REBELLIONS AND ROUGES

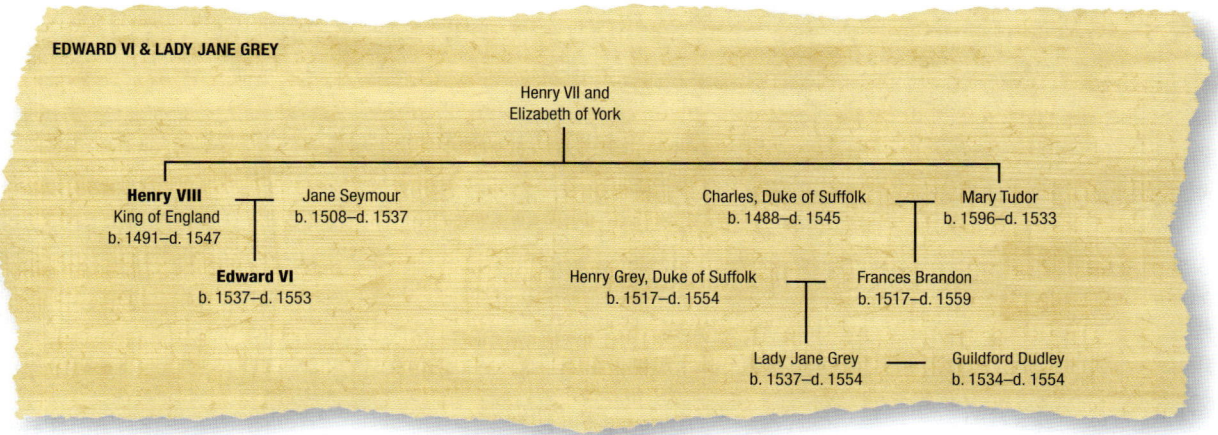

EDWARD VI & LADY JANE GREY

Henry VII and
Elizabeth of York

Henry VIII
King of England
b. 1491–d. 1547

Jane Seymour
b. 1508–d. 1537

Charles, Duke of Suffolk
b. 1488–d. 1545

Mary Tudor
b. 1596–d. 1533

Edward VI
b. 1537–d. 1553

Henry Grey, Duke of Suffolk
b. 1517–d. 1554

Frances Brandon
b. 1517–d. 1559

Lady Jane Grey
b. 1537–d. 1554

Guildford Dudley
b. 1534–d. 1554

King for barely six years, Edward VI did not even reach his majority before he died at the age of 15. The unknown Tudor, Edward was overshadowed by his larger-than-life father, Henry VIII, and his successors Mary I and Elizabeth I. Despite Henry VIII's attempts to secure the throne for his only male heir, Edward VI would face threats to his crown and a reign filled with controversy and unrest.

"Edward VI lived only a few years … but he lived them worthily."

The "godly imp" was led by strong-willed men who became seduced by the thought of absolute power, yet Edward's rule nevertheless cemented

Opposite: Edward VI as painted by Hans Holbein the Younger, circa 1538. The portrait shows the young Edward to be a happy and healthy child. The Latin text at the bottom of the picture encourages Edward to live up to his illustrious father's example.

Protestantism as the new English faith, taking religious reforms further than his father ever intended. However, his ill-timed death left the Tudor monarchy in grave doubt as a succession battle was soon to erupt.

Edward's Childhood
Often described as a happy and lovable child, Edward spent his early childhood among women, who saw to the every want and need of the little prince. Beloved and treated as precious by his father (who, as a young boy, had resented the smothering upbringing of Henry VII and Margaret Beaufort), Edward was

> It is possible that Edward was seen as weak and feeble only in comparison with his gigantic and imposing father.

indulged and cosseted as the son and heir to the King of England, suffering none of the chaos that affected the childhood of both his sisters.

Because of his father's relatively traditional beliefs, Edward's early religious upbringing was largely Catholic. However, after beginning his formal education at the age of six, Edward was given the finest tutors available at the time who were more reformist in their leanings. Richard Cox was Edward's almoner and took a leading role in his education. Cox became an active reformer under Edward's rule. John Cheke was one of Cambridge's brightest students and was responsible for teaching Edward the classics, philosophy and liberal sciences. He also had Protestant beliefs, and the influence of both men would leave a mark on the young King, who, like his father, was eager to appear learned and articulate. Edward was also taught languages, music and arts, as well as foreign affairs and how to behave at court. Unlike Henry VIII—the younger son—there was never any doubt that Edward would grow up to rule his nation and all the signs showed he would make a great King.

Despite views of the prince suffering a weak, unhealthy childhood, Edward enjoyed good health for most of his life, apart from a fever at the age of four. It is believed there were no lasting issues from this childhood malady that may have brought on his early death, although the severe illness might have weakened the young King's constitution. It is possible that Edward was seen as weak and feeble only in comparison with his gigantic and imposing father.

Thought to be close to his older sisters as a child, the young prince enjoyed their visits when the girls were reconciled with their father. It was when Henry VIII married Catherine Parr in 1543 that

Opposite: Crowds have gathered en masse to cheer the coronation procession of the boy king. Edward was crowned on 20 February 1547 at Westminster Abbey, followed by a banquet at Westminster Hall. Six years later, Edward would return to the Abbey to be buried.

the Tudors became a true family. Edward loved the attention of the mother figure he had missed out on (Jane Seymour had died within days of her much-wanted son's birth) and became fond of his sisters, especially Mary.

Henry arranged the betrothal of his son and heir to Mary, Queen of Scots, when Edward was only seven years old. Mary was but seven months at the time. The Treaty of Greenwich was signed in 1543, forming an alliance between the old enemies of England and Scotland that was to be cemented by the marriage. However, by 1547 the betrothal was broken and the Scottish Parliament rejected the Treaty, beginning years of strife known as the "rough wooing." Mary would go on to marry the French Dauphin, later King Francis II of France. With the alliance shattered, England sent troops into Scotland to wage a war that would continue under Edward's reign.

Becoming King

At the tender age of nine, Edward's idyllic childhood came to an abrupt end. His father, the great and notorious Henry VIII, had died. The tragic news was kept secret from the country at first, especially since it had recently undergone such internal religious turmoil, as the idea of a child taking the crown may lead to threats from abroad, as well as possible usurpers looking to snatch the throne from a vulnerable youngster. But Edward was in strong hands. Henry had done all he could to secure his son's succession, leaving his Privy Council in no doubt that Edward, and only Edward, would inherit. If Edward were to die without issue, the crown would revert to Mary, then Elizabeth, Henry having reinstated both daughters as successors in his third Act of Succession in 1543.

Henry had also left the prince's care in the hands of 16 executors and 12 assistants until Edward's

> Henry had done all he could to secure his son's succession, leaving his Privy Council in no doubt that Edward would inherit. If Edward died, the crown would revert to Mary, then Elizabeth …

ROYAL BANQUETS

ALWAYS A SUMPTUOUS affair, Edward's coronation banquet was a sight to behold. Containing every type of meat and fish conceivable, as well as pies, tarts and exotic fruit and vegetables, banquets would typically consist of three to six courses of a large variety of dishes. Food would often be spiced or salted and the nobles would enjoy exotic flavours such as saffron, ginger and cloves. The tables were laid with gold and silver plates. Theatrical centrepieces would resemble swans or peacocks, or represent the coats of arms of attending nobles. While such dinners were a special occasion, there was often a huge amount and variety of food at the King's table. However, the practice would be to sample just a little of your favorite dishes, ensuring that there was enough left to feed the many servants afterwards. Nevertheless, gout was rampant due to the rich food and excessive alcohol consumption.

Other health issues such as vitamin deficiency were also common, as certain foods such as locally grown vegetables were seen as poor people's fare and therefore excluded from banquets.

Above: The spacious size of this Tudor kitchen hints at the huge amounts of food cooked here each day. Fires would be lit in each of the brick ovens on the left of the photo, enabling gallons of soups, stews and sauces to be made at the same time.

18th birthday and majority. Not eager to bequest a single man with the power to manipulate the King, Henry felt that the safest way to protect his legacy was to share it among many. It was also tradition that when a royal in his minority took the throne, little would be done of any consequence by his government until the King came to prominence and could speak for himself, which would give the country time to adjust to a new ruler. Neither precaution was to stand fast. Powerful men with agendas of their own would soon make their own mark on the young monarch and the entire country.

Edward was finally proclaimed King of England on January 31, 1547. His council made the succession a cause for great celebration, hoping to win the support of the public by laying on the expected lavish ceremony for his coronation on February 20. They need not have worried; Edward was already being hailed as the new "Josiah," the Old Testament Hebrew King renowned for reforming Hebrew religion. Cranmer hailed Edward as "Christ's vicar," the personification of Royal Supremacy who was answerable only to God. It was a concept the young sovereign had no trouble believing.

The new King wore red velvet robes trimmed with ermine and the Imperial Crown, now a symbol of both an English King and the Supreme Head of the Church of England. This crown was later replaced with a smaller and lighter crown as a nod to the King's youth, which Edward wore throughout the following banquet. Two cushions were also placed on the seat of the throne to boost Edward's small frame. Edward kept comprehensive diaries throughout his reign, which tell us that one of his lasting memories of the coronation was a tightrope act.

> Benefiting from the "unfulfilled gifts" clause in Henry's will, Seymour won support by awarding himself and his acolytes …

Protector of the Realm

Soon after his coronation, Edward Seymour, the Duke of Somerset, was assigned King Edward's Lord Protector. As the boy's uncle, Seymour was an obvious choice, but others were not so happy about his influential role. Thomas Wriothesley, Earl of Southampton, Lord Chancellor and keeper of the Great Seal—who had earlier been the one to draw up arrest papers for Catherine Parr that Henry then rejected—first refused to grant this authority to Seymour, possibly believing Wriothesley himself should be Protector to the King. Seymour and his cronies quickly put paid to Wriothesley's designs on power

and he resigned, probably to avoid a harsher fate if he did not back down. The old Chancellor would bide his time for now. Seymour later appointed Richard Rich, the lawyer who had testified against Fisher and More, as Lord Chancellor in Wriothesley's place. Benefiting from the "unfulfilled gifts" clause in Henry's will, Seymour won support by awarding himself and his acolytes titles, lands and riches. Many councilmen were more than willing to support him in everything as long as they were compensated for their loyalty.

Now secure in his authority, Seymour basically had control over the King and country. He cemented this control by getting Edward to sign letters patent that gave Seymour the authority to choose Privy Council members, thus enabling him to select like-minded men who owed him. They took advantage of the ambiguity in Henry's will to allow "unfulfilled gifts" to be distributed, which ended up with each of Seymour's supporters gaining titles and lands. Around this time, the more conservative men of court fell out of favor. This included Thomas Howard, who had been a favorite of Henry's for a large part of his reign and who would later serve Elizabeth, and Stephen Gardiner. A conservative Catholic, Gardiner would remain a source of opposition to Seymour's intended religious reforms, which went further than Henry VIII had ever wanted. With the speedy removal of these men, plus placing his supporters within Edward's household so the Lord Protector could even control who saw the King, Seymour's takeover of Edward was smooth, deadly efficient and practically unchallenged.

Brotherly Love

Thomas Seymour, Edward's younger brother, was not happy with the control Seymour had over Edward, wanting more authority of his own. Fighting for absolute power over the susceptible monarch, Thomas did his best to destroy Seymour's authority. Thomas held the titles of Duke of Somerset as a consequence of the "unfulfilled gifts" clause, which Seymour hoped would be enough to buy him off. Thomas was also Lord High Admiral and a member of the Privy Council. However, instead of directly challenging

Left: This dramatic illustration shows an angry Thomas Seymour trying to force his way into Edward's quarters at Hampton Court. The barking dog alerted the guards, who quickly dealt with Thomas. His brother, Edward Seymour, was Edward's protector.

War at Pinkie Cleugh

The final weeks of Henry VIII's life were tumultuous, due to the on-again, off-again battles with Scotland. The continued attempts—with future good relations hopefully secured by Edward's marriage to Mary, Queen of Scots—at peace being thwarted, the "rough wooing" of Scotland commenced. Part of the dispute was England wanting to force reformation on the largely Catholic population of Scotland. Seymour also wanted to secure the English borders against a possible Scottish–French invasion. The Protector and warlord

Part of the dispute was England wanting to force reformation on the largely Catholic population of Scotland.

Below: This striking image depicts the Battle of Pinkie Cleugh, near Musselburgh in the south-east of Scotland. Part of the "rough wooing," the battle saw the Scots defeated by the English.

Left: Henry II of France supported the "Auld Alliance" with Scotland against England. Cementing this alliance, his son, Francis II, married Mary Queen of Scots in 1558.

used their weapons to great effect against them. Seymour left men in Scotland, which he believed would keep the peace and ensure English authority across the border, but this, plus the costly wars, would cause a huge financial drain that Seymour was later criticized for. However, Scotland, then under the regency of James Hamilton, the Earl of Arran, after James V's death in 1542, still refused to capitulate. In August 1548 Mary was smuggled to safety in France where she would later marry Francis II and briefly act as Queen Consort. The Treaty was broken and the war had been for nothing.

Mary, Queen of Scots' mother, Mary of Guise, was a dominant figure in the Anglo–Scottish negotiations, replacing Hamilton as her daughter's Regent in 1554. While assuring Henry that the marriage between Mary and Prince Edward would go ahead when Mary was ten, she kept up negotiations with France to ensure that her daughter was safe from the tempestuous English King. It is rumored that Mary of Guise had herself refused an offer of becoming Henry's sixth wife, fearing for the state of her neck!

The resulting war hit the King's depleted coffers hard, running into what would today be hundreds of millions. Seymour took steps to gain money by

> It is rumored that Mary of Guise had herself refused an offer of becoming Henry's sixth wife, fearing for the state of her neck!

led his army into Scotland on August 31, 1547. With an offer of peace on the condition of the marriage going ahead being rejected, the English routed the Scots in an overwhelming defeat with over 10,000 Scots killed at Pinkie, near Edinburgh. The Scots attacked, but their troops were split and the more modern English army

Opposite: This portrait of Mary of Guise, the wife of James V of Scotland, shows her to be a strong and determined woman. Mary later became Regent of Scotland, but her Catholic beliefs were the cause of dissent with the growing number of Protestants in Scotland.

A combination of religious reforms, unpopular decisions and public rebellions heightened the tension in England.

debasing the pound, the effect of which would cause inflation and financial hardship for many of Edward's subjects. Seymour also set up the enclosures initiative, which had a profound affect on land ownership and caused widespread fears of possible abuses. Things were unravelling fast for Seymour. A combination of religious reforms, unpopular decisions and public rebellions heightened the tension in England. Events came to a head in 1549 and brought about the beginning of the end for Seymour, with outbreaks of rebellion and violence occurring across the realm.

Troubles in France

As well as quashing the Scots, Edward and his protectors had to deal with attacks from France. Francis I died in April 1547 and was succeeded by his son, Henry II (Francis II's father). Henry II was eager to support the "auld alliance" with Scotland as well as getting the English out of Boulogne, which he wanted to take back for France. While Seymour had the support of Charles V, the Holy Roman Emperor would only intervene if Calais (still under English rule) was attacked. Then, in 1549, Henry II's fleet set sail for England on the attack but were beaten back around Jersey by the superior English Navy. Dudley later negotiated with Henry II to sell Boulogne back to France, upholding the two countries' original settlement.

Kett's Rebellion

Originating in Wymondham, Norfolk, the rebellion started as a protest against the enclosure of sections of land in England. These enclosures meant that certain parcels of land were worth a lot more money than others. The enclosed land could be used for rearing

Opposite: Catherine de Medici was the wife of Henry II of France. While she was largely sidelined by Henry's lover, Diane de Poitiers, throughout his lifetime, Catherine could be ruthless and closely supervised each of her three sons during their time as ruler of France.

sheep for the increasingly affluent wool trade. It also meant that less land was available for growing crops at a time when inflation and the population were rising quickly and food would often run short. Minor rumblings of unrest first broke out across the country in 1548, the root cause of which was a religious dispute, social unrest and the enclosures law. Many men involved literally had nothing better to do as their source of livelihood had been robbed. These upsurges of discontent may have inspired Robert Kett and his followers.

Seymour, sensing the unpopularity of the laws, ordered an enquiry but it was predominantly led by landowners who benefitted from the enclosures rule. Unsurprisingly, they ruled it to be fair practice. When the fences put up by some of the more wealthy landowners were kicked down, Robert Kett, himself a landowner, joined the rebels and led them into further revolt. Their numbers quickly building to thousands, they stormed Norwich—then England's second largest city—demanding a halt to these unwanted practices.

Robert Kett had previously supported the commoners when their village church was threatened with being torn down. Kett now took their side again and organized the disgruntled rebels into a coherent mass. From their camp at Mousehold Heath near Norwich they drew up a list of grievances, which was sent to Seymour in July 1549. But the rebels received a tough response—their demands would not be met. They were ordered to disband immediately or face arrest. However, if they did disperse the uprisers would all be pardoned. Refusing, Kett's men stayed put, with the King's enforcers—who had not expected refusal—having no way of forcing their removal.

Forced into movement, Kett and his followers attacked Norwich. William Parr, the Marquess of Northampton, was sent with troops to force an end

... the rebellion started as a protest against the enclosure of sections of land ... It also meant that less land was available for growing crops at a time when inflation and the population were rising quickly ...

Above: This illustration shows Kett's Rebellion of 1549. Trees often appear in images of the Rebellion, signifying Kett's Tree of Reformation on Mousehold Heath, under which the rebels held their camp.

thousands already dead, 300 men were executed for their part in the rebellion. No reforms were made and the end result was merely to weaken Seymour's hold over the King and council.

Below: Kett and his followers believed they were acting for the King, who was being mislead by his advisors with agendas of their own. However, a royal proclamation was issued against the rebels to quash the disturbance.

to the rebellion. However, Kett and his men met the challenge, forcing Northampton to retreat. Seymour then sent in John Dudley and a far greater force to impose order. Faced with a vastly increased army, the rioters found their position weakened and their supply lines cut off. Sensing their defeat, Kett wanted to discuss terms with Dudley, but the rebellion was now to end in bloodshed. Kett's men fought bravely for their cause, but eventually the superior might and weaponry of Dudley's army proved too much. Up to 2000 of the rebels were killed, with many more fleeing for their lives. Kett was captured and taken to the Tower. He was returned to Norwich in December 1549, where he was hanged from the castle walls as a warning to others. There his body remained until his rotting flesh started peeling from his bones. In addition to the

Sensing their defeat, Kett wanted to discuss terms with Dudley, but the rebellion was now to end in bloodshed … eventually the superior might and weaponry of Dudley's army proved too much.

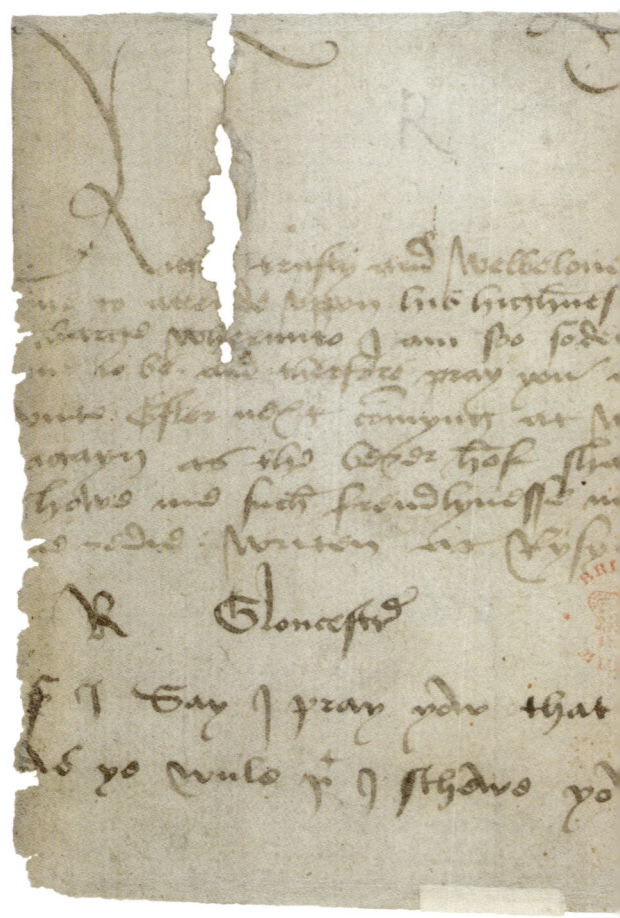

Backing Mary

As strict reforms were closely followed by such rebellions, support for Mary to take over as monarch in the place of the young King was rising. Mary continued to hear mass in Latin and even offered a general invitation for anyone who wanted to join her at mass to do so on Whitsun in 1548, the very day of enforcement of Cranmer's English mass. Her open devotion to the traditional Catholic faith meant that conservatives who thought Edward's advisors had gone too far were more open about defying the new reforms. If Mary could see her own brother as a heretic, so could her supporters! Many also feared for their very souls, as the reforms embracing faith and devotion were all very well, but years of Catholic doctrine had taught people there was more to securing a place in heaven than faith alone.

> Mary continued to hear mass in Latin and even offered a general invitation for anyone who wanted to join her.

Eager to escape the possible fires of hell, the public saw Mary as their savior, a role she would later take to heart. In addition, many superstitious people saw the bad harvests and lack of food and money as signs from God.

During a family gathering for Christmas 1550, Edward—then aged 13—would reduce Mary to tears as he berated her heretical ways. With both siblings as

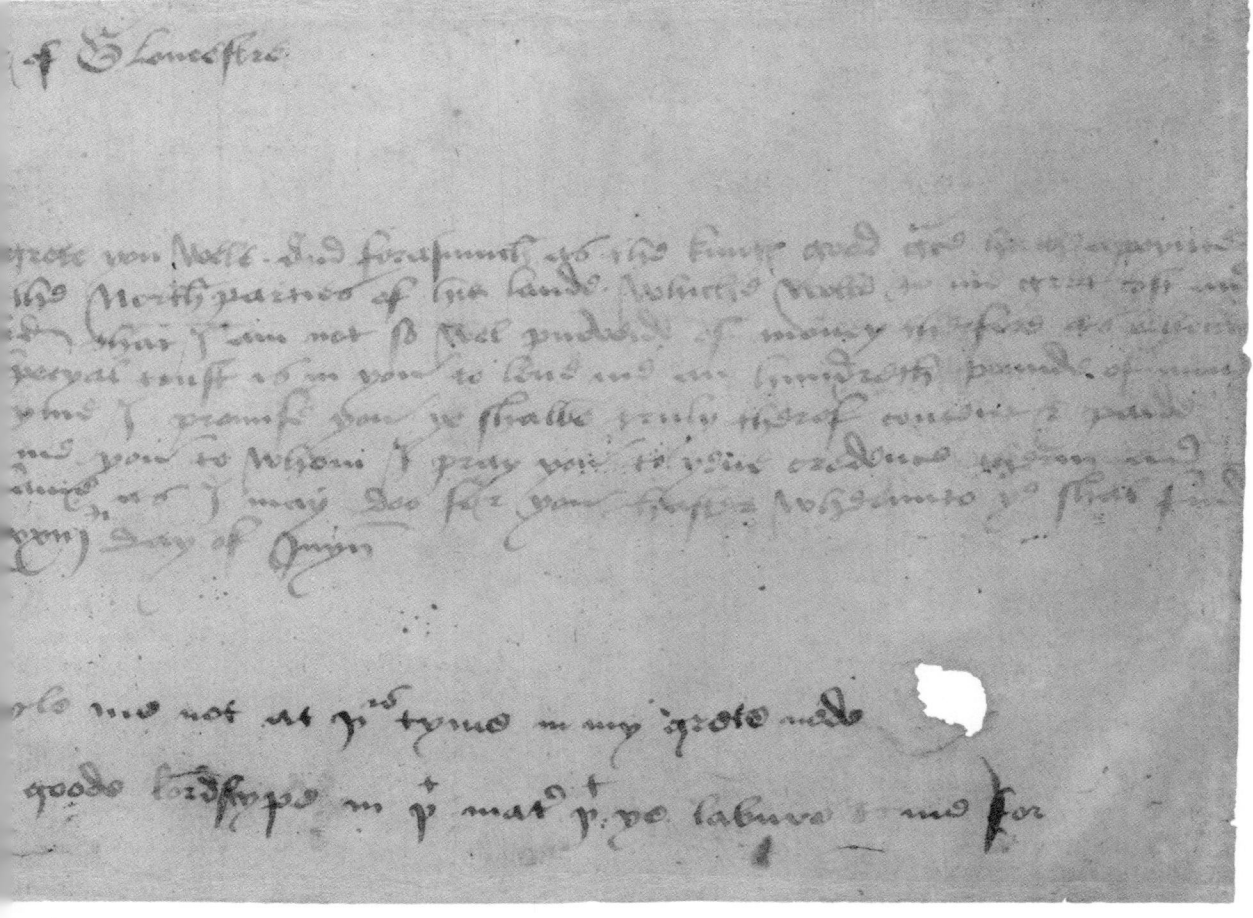

stubborn as each other, it would later be Edward in tears of frustration as Mary called on the support of her powerful cousin, Charles V.

Seymour's Fall and Dudley's Rise

These catastrophic and violent events were blamed largely on Seymour's mishandling of affairs and his efforts to feather his own nest. With even his old friends and supporters turning against him, Seymour faced a serious challenge to his title of Protector. Panicking, he took Edward to Windsor Castle on October 7, keeping the King, now 12 years old, a virtual prisoner. The council took steps to remove Seymour's powers and he was arrested on October 11, 1549. Edward was returned to power—although still in his minority— and Seymour was sent to the Tower in disgrace. John Dudley took control of the monarch. Edward was returned to safety and councilmen approved by Dudley had to be with him at all times.

Seymour, by this time locked deep within the belly of the Tower, signed articles of submission in the hope of winning back his freedom and authority. He was later pardoned and reconciled to Dudley in February 1550, when Dudley was made Lord President of the Council and was sure of his authority. Later trying to usurp Dudley's new power, Seymour was arrested for treason on October 16 and executed on January 22, 1552. Dudley later admitted that many of the charges were fabricated.

Dudley was now firmly in charge of the young King.

Good Duke, Bad Duke

The similarities between both of Edward's protectors are many, despite the well-known presentation of Seymour as the "good duke" and Dudley as the "bad duke." As we have seen, both were self-serving, ambitious and manipulative. Seymour was seen as arrogant, largely ignoring the council and ruling through proclamations. Dudley is thought to have set brother against brother, knowing that both Seymour brothers wanted to use their family connection to gain authority over the boy. His machinations certainly led to discord between them.

However, Dudley is also thought to have acted out of fear for his family and it could be argued that Seymour was doing his best to leave Edward with a strong country, united under a single religion that Edward fervently believed in. Another interesting note is that under Seymour's protectorate, there were no

Above: As well-meaning as Edward Seymour insisted he had been, the Lord Protector was executed at Tower Hill in 1552. By this time, Dudley, his rival for power, had already supplanted his role as protector.

religious executions for heresy. It was also here that the 1414 Act for the Burning of Heretics was removed from statute law.

It is true that life settled down somewhat under Dudley. He avoided war with France by negotiating the return of Boulogne in 1550. The wars and rebellions were over and England would soon have a King able to rule his own country. For a brief time in 1552, it looked as if peace would persevere. Little did anyone foresee the turbulent years that lay ahead.

In 1552, Dudley started preparing Edward for his majority reign. He also negotiated with Henry II of France for Edward to marry Elisabeth of Valois, Henry's daughter, to secure peace between England and France. Edward's death would render these negotiations moot and Elisabeth would later marry

Later trying to usurp Dudley's new power, Seymour was arrested for treason on October 16 and executed on January 22, 1552. Dudley later admitted that many of the charges were fabricated.

JOHN DUDLEY

JOHN DUDLEY WAS the son of Edmund Dudley, Henry VII's financial advisor who was executed as a scapegoat by Henry VIII. He was a powerful, charismatic man who was loyal to whoever sat on the throne. This has resulted in depictions of him as hypocritical and cynical, not having any strong faith of his own. His Machiavellian part in the "Devise for the Succession" making Lady Jane Grey (who would soon become his daughter-in-law) Queen shows his lust for power. There are even rumors that Dudley hastened Edward's death by poisoning him. Dudley's downfall mirrored his father's, despite all his attempts to hold on to power by pleasing the current monarch. Deeply hated towards the end of his life, Dudley was arrested and taken to the Tower before being executed on August 22, 1553 (illustrated below).

Philip II of Spain after Mary I's death in 1558. Edward started to sit in on council meetings more regularly and started signing royal warrants in his own hand. Even though he was only 13 years old it was easy to see that Edward shared his father's expectation of being obeyed. Had Edward reached his majority, he would likely have made a forcible and effective monarch. But less than a year later, Edward was dead.

Contracting measles in April 1552, Edward was very ill for several months. He did start to make a recovery and even went on procession around the country over the summer to tour his realm and get to know his country. However, by Christmas on 1552, the young King was seriously ill. Edward grew worse over the next few months, making his decision about his successor vitally important.

Passing on the Crown

However much Edward was led by strong, manipulative men, he was his father's son. Edward knew his own mind and expected others to give him what he wanted. The reforms made in England throughout his minority reign were supported by him, even done on his say so. Edward's succession laws prove that he did what he could to prevent a Catholic Queen ruling his country and overturning these reforms, even if this Queen was his beloved sister.

Below: John Dudley is often seen as a villain in comparison to Seymour, but history suggests that both men sought power over the boy king. Dudley did not live long after Edward's death.

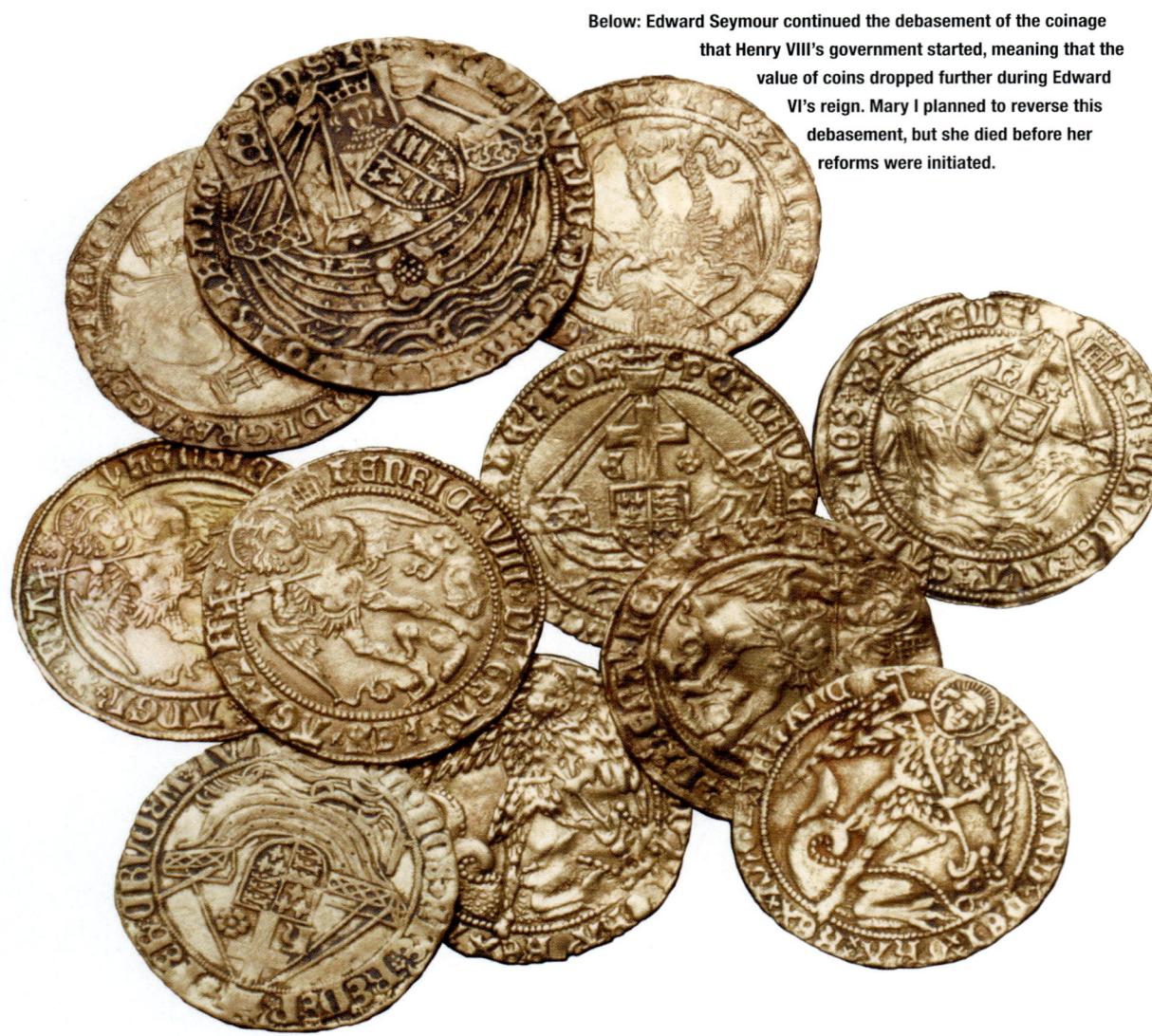

What was right and good—in his eyes—was right and good for everyone, especially a woman who had been made a bastard.

As Edward's current successor was his sister Mary, neither he nor his council were content with leaving England under the control of a single, Catholic female. Edward drafted his "Devise for the Succession" in May 1553, which bypassed both Mary and Elizabeth—it not being possible to disinherit Mary and not her sister—leaving the country in the hands of Lady Jane Grey until such time as she was to produce male heirs. Jane Grey was the granddaughter of Henry VIII's sister, Mary Tudor, and Charles Brandon, whose father had been Henry VII's standard-bearer. William Brandon had died at the hand of Richard III at Bosworth Field, ostensibly saving Henry VII's life. Having Jane Grey as his successor would leave the crown in the hands of a Tudor descendant who would both continue the family line and uphold the Protestant beliefs that were so important to Edward.

MONEY MATTERS

BEGINNING UNDER HENRY VIII and continuing in earnest under Edward VI, the debasement of the currency hit new lows. This meant that more coins could be made, making extra coinage for the government, but they would not be worth so much when in use. Continued debasement also meant that prices and inflation shot up and trade with England from foreign countries declined.

Originally being made of fine silver, the 9.25 silver sterling coins were introduced in 1158.

By Edward's rule, silver coins were made up of only one-third silver, the rest being cheaper metals, meaning that their value had dropped significantly. The coins themselves were said to blush in embarrassment, with the pinkish copper literally shining through the silver.

How far John Dudley manipulated Edward is unknown, but it was the spring of 1553—after Edward had first fallen ill—that Dudley proposed the union between his son, Guildford, and Jane Grey. They were married on May 25 that same year, although Jane did deny her husband the crown matrimonial, limiting his influence as King. While the Succession originally ruled that only Jane's male children could be heirs to the throne, the will was changed so that Jane herself could be crowned Queen. At only 16 or 17 years old, she would have been easy to control through her husband and father-in-law, leaving the crown effectively in Dudley's grasping hands.

Edward's Devise contravened Henry VIII's third Act of Succession, which named both his daughters as successors should Edward die without leaving a male heir, effectively making it against statute law. However, Edward excluded them both on the grounds of illegitimacy, Henry carelessly never renouncing his daughters' legitimacy before his death. Edward's will was passed by the council with Dudley ensuring that everyone signed it. Dudley even kept tight control over who visited the ailing King, not letting either Mary or Elizabeth speak to Edward prior to his death should they change his mind.

Edward addressed his public for the final time on July 1, 1553. The crowds were appalled by his wasted, frail appearance. He was now in pain, finding it hard to stand and breathe. Edward died five days later on

> Edward drafted his "Devise for the Succession" in May 1553, which bypassed both Mary and Elizabeth … leaving the country in the hands of Lady Jane Grey until such time as she was to produce male heirs.

July 6, the actual cause of his death being unknown, possibly tuberculosis. He joined his ancestors in Henry VII's Lady Chapel in Westminster Abbey, the trusted Cranmer performing the young King's funeral rites.

Things might have turned out very differently if Mary had not been allowed to leave London for East Anglia, which enabled her to raise sympathy and forces. Any progress made during Edward's brief reign was soon to be wiped out as Mary supplanted her own dominance over her council and country. And what of the Nine Days' Queen? A vulnerable pawn who would be executed before she reached the age of 20, Jane Grey was initially spared execution by Mary and remained a prisoner in the Tower, to which she was taken to be crowned Queen of England and would never leave. Only after the Wyatt Rebellion, where Jane might have been used as a figurehead to supplant

LADY JANE GREY

JANE WAS—UNDERSTANDABLY—VERY NERVOUS prior to her execution on February 12, 1554. She stressed her innocence of plots to depose Mary right up to the end and her last moments were filled with confusion and terror. Jane was blindfolded, as was traditional, and needed help finding her way to the block. Pardoning the executioner for his crime of taking her life, Jane asked for a speedy dispatch in return.

Praying for God to take her soul, the Nine Days' Queen breathed her last. Her execution was depicted by Paul Delaroche in *The Execution of Lady Jane Grey* (1833), now hanging in London's National Gallery. It shows her feeling for the block, with one of her faithful ladies-in-waiting swooning with grief in the background.

> … following Edward's death … Religious beliefs were in chaos, with no one knowing quite where to turn. People of both Catholic and Protestant faiths were equally likely to be charged with heresy.

Mary, did Jane's death become more of a necessity—she was executed along with her husband and father.

It is interesting to speculate how England would have been different had Edward not died so young. With both his intelligence and authority increasing during his final years, Edward had learned much from his protectors and had the makings of a great and powerful King. Under his authority, England may have prospered and Protestantism may have extended across Europe. Chances are his heirs would have succeeded him, meaning that neither Mary nor Elizabeth would ever be able to make their mark as English monarch. But this was not to be. The sorry state of affairs following Edward's death left England in turmoil. Religious beliefs were in chaos, with no one knowing quite where to turn. People of both Catholic and Protestant faiths were equally likely to be charged with heresy. The country was poor and many feared invasion from abroad. Switching back to Catholicism under Mary I was about to result in the infamous Bloody Mary burning over 280 martyrs at the stake. The first Queen of England was about to make her mark in blood and fire.

Below: Signed "Jane the Quene," this letter was written by Lady Jane Grey to William Parr. It asks for Parr's support against Mary. One wonders how much of the letter was written by Jane herself.

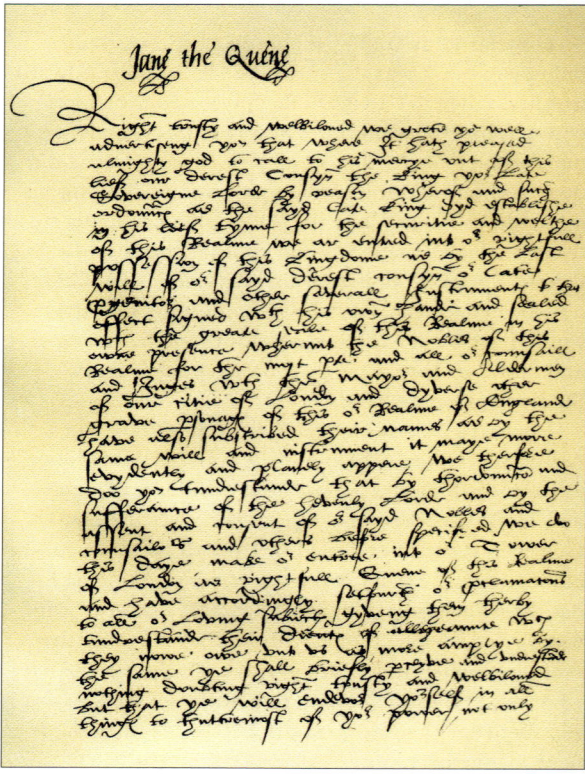

Opposite: This image of Jane Grey shows a docile young girl. However, as Queen, Jane may well have dispensed with the conniving Seymour, having already refused his son (her husband) the title of king.

MARY, MARY, QUITE CONTRARY

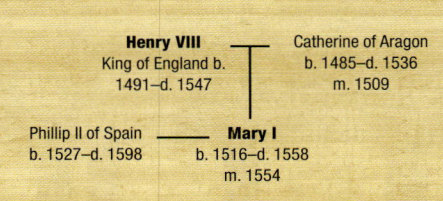

Henry VIII
King of England b.
1491–d. 1547

Catherine of Aragon
b. 1485–d. 1536
m. 1509

Phillip II of Spain
b. 1527–d. 1598

Mary I
b. 1516–d. 1558
m. 1554

To great adulation, Mary I began her reign as the beloved savior of traditional religion in England. However, her five-year rule would see deaths, famine, war, martyrs and rebellion that led to England's first Queen being one of the most abhorred English monarchs in history.

"If God be for us, who can be against us?"—Mary I

Mary's determination to restore the Tudor line to its rightful religion saw her overturn reforms set in motion by her father and brother, make an ill-advised foreign marriage, suffer illness and false pregnancies and leave her country worse off for her efforts. Bloody Mary would go from being hailed as the nation's redeemer to dying estranged from her husband and sister, childless and reviled.

Opposite: Pictured here looking pensive, the first crowned Queen of England had much to endure throughout her life, from being disowned by her father at the age of 17 to suffering several false pregnancies during her miserable marriage to Philip II of Spain.

Henry's Heir

Being the firstborn child of the King was never easy for a daughter. Mary suffered more than most as she went from being the adored heir to the English throne to an unwanted bastard while still a teenager. This tumultuous childhood affected her deeply and conferred on Mary the character traits that would mar her later reign. As Henry's first surviving child, Mary was revered and adored. As a daughter, she was tolerated until a son came along. When Catherine of Aragon was Queen, Mary was the beloved successor to the throne. When Anne Boleyn was Queen, Mary was declared baseborn and feared for her life.

Brought up a devout Catholic, Mary later had to deny her beliefs and turn to the Church of England to appease her father, the man who had discarded her as illegitimate and destroyed her much-loved mother's happiness. The pattern of her life was to lose anything

Right: This picture shows an ornate example of a virginal, a harpsichord-like instrument very popular in Tudor times. Both Mary and Elizabeth were keen players and the attractive example shown here actually belonged to Elizabeth.

> The pretty princess was also useful in cementing alliances— Mary was betrothed several times during her childhood …

of importance. It was a pattern that would reoccur even when she was Queen. Mary was never able to shake off the bonds of blood, which affected her both physically and mentally throughout her chaotic life.

Born in 1516, for the first few years of her life Mary was beloved of both parents. Catherine of Aragon, Mary's mother, had several miscarriages before managing to carry Mary to term. While Henry VIII was disappointed that she had not been a boy, Mary was seen as evidence that he would soon bear a son. Henry was fond of the young princess. Mary displayed remarkable skills in music and language and was well

educated, her parents proud of her intelligence and perspicacity. The pretty princess was also useful in cementing alliances—Mary was betrothed several times during her childhood in the hope of forging strong alliances within Europe.

Lady Mary

When the princess was 17 years old, her life would change forever. Henry had fallen in love and was determined to rid himself of Catherine. Her father's arrogant and autocratic nature meant that he discarded his wife and daughter without a second thought. Annulling the marriage meant that Mary had to be disowned. Henry was so sure of his ability to produce male heirs that he cast Mary aside with her now-useless mother. Now "Lady Mary," she was quickly supplanted by her half-sister Elizabeth, the daughter of Anne Boleyn. Anne's manipulative self-interest saw Mary sent away from court in isolation, removed from anyone sympathetic towards her. She became one of

Elizabeth's ladies-in-waiting, a role not fitting for a princess but suitable for a lady.

Anne was convinced that as the eldest child, Mary would one day succeed to the throne and overthrow Elizabeth. This fear may have spurred Henry, previously Mary's devoted father, to push his eldest daughter into acknowledging Anne as Queen and her children as the rightful heirs, meaning that she accepted her own illegitimacy. For Mary, this would also mean conceding that the marriage of her dear mother was unlawful and false.

Henry's break with the Church of Rome was the cause of much anguish for Mary, who was under great pressure to recognize Henry as Supreme Head of the Church of England, as well as denouncing the office of the Pope. Lady Mary expressed her stubborn and

BLESSING OF THE BED

A CUSTOM FROM medieval times was to bless the marital bed of the happy couple on the day of their wedding. Based on the Sarum Rites—a form of worship based itself on the traditional Roman Church ceremony, which Mary revived under her rule—on the evening of the wedding, the priest would come to the marriage bed with the bride and groom (plus various well-wishers). He would bless the room, bed and couple, asking God to watch over them. The blessing was especially important when the couple needed to procreate successfully. The curtains around the bed would then be shut to afford some privacy, but trusted servants would often remain in the room to ensure the man did his duty! The bloodied sheets of the marriage consummation were sometimes even kept as proof of the union.

Below: The queen's private bedchamber at Hampton Court Palace.

Opposite: Mary is often pictured looking serious and devout. Note the crucifix around her neck, a visible sign of her strong Catholic beliefs, worn even when she had to keep on the right side of her father.

spirited nature here by flat-out refusing to submit to her father's demands. Henry maliciously banned Mary and Catherine from seeing each other, showing no sympathy even though both suffered from ill health throughout this time. But even this punishment would not soften Mary's resolve. It was only when her cousin, Charles V, persuaded her to capitulate that Mary gave in and made the acknowledgements Henry demanded. This decision would haunt Mary for the rest of her life.

Growing Up at Court

Mary was soon reconciled to her fickle father, despite Anne's hostility towards her, and returned to life at court. Her situation improved when Anne was executed and Henry married Jane Seymour, who sought to further reunite father and daughter. Mary also soon had company in her illegitimate status when Henry passed his second Act of Succession in 1536 to ensure that any children he had with Jane became heir to the throne over both daughters. Henry was finally rewarded with the son he so desired and Mary again became a useful bargaining tool as a bride, even though she was now 21 years old and certainly less acquiescent than she used to be.

Still charming and pretty, Mary was courted by Philip, Duke of Bavaria, but his Lutheran beliefs made his advances intolerable. Thomas Cromwell then proposed a match between Mary and the Duke of Cleves, eager to ally England to Germany in the face of hostility from Rome and the Catholic countries of

Left: Another common pose for Mary shows her at prayer. This engraving captures her committed nature and hints at the determination with which she would enforce religious doctrine on England, an action that Mary thought would save the souls of her people.

> … Edward VI … felt he could not make Mary or Elizabeth his heir as they were not legally Henry's children. However, the main issue for Edward was Mary's ardent Catholic beliefs.

Europe. In the end this came to nothing, but was the cause of Cromwell's downfall after he engineered the marriage of Henry VIII to Anne of Cleves, the Duke's homely sister. Mary would act as Henry's hostess between his marriages, being an accomplished dancer

as well as a skilled musician. It was during Henry's sixth marriage to Catherine Parr that Mary enjoyed closer relations with her father, sister and brother. Henry even restored Mary and Elizabeth to the line of succession in 1544, although both daughters remained illegitimate in the eyes of the law.

This would be a sticky issue under Edward VI, who felt he could not make Mary or Elizabeth his heir as they were not legally Henry's children. However, the main issue for Edward was Mary's ardent Catholic beliefs.

Below: Mary is here crowned Queen Mary I of England. At the beginning of her reign, Mary was a far more popular choice than Lady Jane Grey. However, the eager crowds that can be seen cheering her coronation soon turned against her violent and irrational acts.

MARIA Catholische in Engeland.

A Strong Faith

Brother and sister were equally obstinate and
convinced of their own righteousness. Unfortunately,
their opinions on religious righteousness were opposite,
which meant that no matter how much affection had
once been between them, they could never truly be
friends. Mary absolutely refused to turn her back on
Catholicism, even while Edward and his advisors were
pushing to make Henry's Church of England far more
Protestant. Edward saw it as heresy that Mary still took
the mass in Latin and followed Catholic doctrine. She
flouted him further by inviting his subjects to join her
in open worship. The only concession Mary made—
when believing herself to be in real danger—was to
hold her beloved mass in private.

Mary even toyed with the idea of fleeing from
England to Brussels, where she could practice her faith
without fear. She was guided by her cousin, Charles V,
whom she often sought for help and advice. So strong
was their relationship that Charles had a guiding hand
in her later marriage to his son, Philip II of Spain.
Mary also asked Charles to bring his might against a
heretical England and forcibly restore the country to its
Catholic faith.

WOMEN IN POWER

A FEMALE MONARCH was almost unheard of and
certainly unprecedented (although Matilda, Henry I's
daughter and Lady Jane Grey were both proclaimed
Queen, although neither were crowned). Indeed, Salic
law in France even forbade women to reign. While
no such law applied to Mary, a female ruler was hard
for many to take and was exactly what Henry VII and
Henry VIII had been eager to avoid. Was a woman
able to govern her nation with the same authority as a
man, in the face of possible rebellion, war or unrest?
Could a weak and emotional woman ever be as strong
as a man? There was also a practical issue. On her
marriage, the Queen would be giving authority to
her husband, so fears of a love marriage rather than a
political union was cause for concern.

Mary was able to silence many fears. She ruled
with authority and majesty—in a style reminiscent
of her father—and had the influence to turn the
tide of Protestantism back, restoring the country to
Catholicism. However, Mary also confirmed some of
these reservations. She believed herself to be in love
with Prince Philip of Spain after merely seeing his
portrait, which led to the ill-advised marriage and
potential of a foreigner taking the English throne. Her
desire for a child resulted in false pregnancies that saw
her ridiculed and pitied throughout Europe, and her
single-minded religion blinkered her to the harm she
caused her country and own reputation. It would be
Elizabeth turning away from such female traits that
would somewhat restore the balance.

**Right: The Great Seal
of Queen Mary I.**

> Lady Jane Grey … was the granddaughter of Henry VIII's sister Mary, whom Edward had chosen because her male heirs would carry on the Tudor line and because of her Protestant beliefs.

Always popular with her countrymen, Mary had a devoted following who were eager to see her ascend to the throne in place of Edward, whose reforms under Seymour were becoming more and more intolerable. One of the demands of the Pilgrimage of Grace under Henry VIII was that Mary be restored to legitimacy. It would be these devoted followers who supported Mary on Edward's death.

Replacing Lady Jane

While Mary would tolerate her brother ruling over her, despite his minority, it was an insult that she had been passed over in favor of her second cousin, Lady Jane Grey. Jane was the granddaughter of Henry VIII's sister Mary, whom Edward had chosen because her male heirs would carry on the Tudor line and because of her Protestant beliefs. Edward was confident that Jane would not undo his reforms, which he was equally sure that Mary would do away with the first chance she got. But the King's will was not to be. Mary would soon be crowned the first Queen of England at Westminster Abbey.

The country had spoken. As soon as Edward was on the brink of death, Mary fled to East Anglia. She had been advised of a plot to remove her so that Jane Grey's accession would not be obstructed. Mary also knew there was no way she could convince Edward—the intractable brother so like herself and their father— that the crown should pass to her. But that no longer mattered. Mary had the majority of the public on her side and God in her corner. Her support had been growing for years and was most buoyant in East Anglia,

Left: Mary I is seen here on her triumphant return to London to claim her rightful throne. In this sumptuous painting, Mary receives blessings from her supporters. Princess Elizabeth stands just behind her, not looking best pleased at the attention bestowed on Mary!

Above: This painting of Lady Jane Grey's execution depicts the would-be queen as young and innocent, further highlighting the tragedy of her final years and death. Despite her youth, Jane was a strong Protestant and refused to convert to Catholicism before her death.

> Lady Jane Grey … was proclaimed Queen … Having no official coronation, Jane was famously ruler of England for only nine days.

the area that had been so harshly repressed during Kett's Rebellion. From her safe house, Mary wrote to the Privy Council of her intent to succeed Edward as the rightful Tudor heir.

Despite this, Lady Jane Grey—a political pawn used by Dudley and his cronies—was proclaimed Queen on August 10. Having no official coronation, Jane

was famously ruler of England for only nine days. It took Mary a matter of days to gather a large crowd of supporters. As her army grew, any remaining support for Jane faded away. Without even having to come to blows with Dudley's troops (many of whom soon defected to Mary's army), Mary and her supporters managed to depose the Nine Days' Queen and imprison her in the Tower, along with her husband, Guildford, and his father, Dudley, who was executed on August 22, 1553.

Protestant leaders were given a
choice of exile to another
country, reconciliation to
Catholicism or punishment.
It is thought that around 800
people left England under Mary …

One of her very first acts was to free her Catholic supporters from the Tower, namely Stephen Gardiner, Edmund Bonner and Thomas Howard. Gardiner became Bishop of Winchester again and was given a seat on Mary's council (still filled with Protestant men after Edward's reign). It was Gardiner who presided over Mary's coronation on October 1, 1553. Never as bloodthirsty as her father, despite her infamous nickname, Mary was loath to execute Jane, whom she saw as innocent and manipulated.

Mary: The Monarch

Mary was eager to reunite England with the Catholic Church. She made immediate steps towards this by calling Parliament on October 5. The council, as well as proclaiming her parents' marriage valid, pronounced that any religious reforms made under Edward's reign were to be abolished. Despite Mary saying that she would move with caution and that her subjects would not be forced to follow Catholicism, it soon became clear that the new Queen was just as dogmatic as her brother. Influential Protestant leaders were silenced or imprisoned, and Mary quickly returned doctrine to the point of the 1539 Act of Six Articles. This meant that priests who had married were now guilty of committing an offense. From December 20, 1553 it became illegal to take part in a Protestant mass, and the Latin mass was reinstated.

There was now a quandary over what to do with Church lands. Purchased by wealthy nobles who had no intention of giving them up, Mary had to reach an agreement with the council and Church over ownership. In the end, profit won out over good intentions and the lands remained private property.

Contrary to popular belief, Mary was not keen to cause people suffering. In her early years as Queen there had to be a good reason for her to condemn

Above: Stephen Gardiner was Bishop of Winchester and Mary's Lord Chancellor. Gardiner had been involved in Henry VIII's annulment from Catherine of Aragon. Despite this, he and Mary fervently agreed on religion and Gardiner crowned Mary during her coronation.

anyone to death. Protestant leaders were given a choice of exile to another country, reconciliation to Catholicism or punishment. It is thought that around 800 people left England under Mary to avoid this punishment and maintain their Protestant faith.

One exception to Mary's magnanimous nature was Thomas Cranmer. Here, the bile ran deep. Not only had Cranmer been integral in propagating

> Cranmer went as far as accepting papal supremacy and transubstantiation, which he had personally branded heresy.

Protestantism to an extreme level, it had also been Cranmer who pronounced Henry and Catherine's marriage null and void, leaving Henry free to cast Mary and Catherine aside. This was a sin that Mary was not willing to pardon and is an example of how determined she could be. Believing that God had made her Queen to restore the country to its state of grace, Mary saw herself as saving souls instead of making martyrs.

Cranmer stood trial for treason on November 13, 1553 and was found guilty. He languished in prison until another trial commenced in 1554. It was not until he had watched Latimer and Ridley being burned at the stake that Cranmer recanted, eventually making several repudiations of his Protestant beliefs, saying that he had turned back to Catholicism. Cranmer went as far as accepting papal supremacy and transubstantiation, which he had personally branded heresy. Technically, Mary no longer had grounds with which to execute Cranmer. Ignoring a further

Below: Cranmer plunges his right hand into the flames that lick around his body, fulfilling a promise he made on the day he died: "forasmuch as my hand hath offended ... therefore my hand shall first be punished; for when I come to the fire it shall first be burned."

REGINALD POLE

REGINALD POLE WAS the third son of Margaret Pole, the Countess of Salisbury. Margaret was Mary's governess and her fortunes often followed those of Mary. Reginald had served Henry VIII prior to Mary, but fell out of favor when he refused to support Henry's divorce from Catherine. Henry took harsh revenge by executing members of his family, and Pole was exiled until 1554.

He was briefly considered as a potential suitor of Mary's before being made the last ever Catholic Archbishop of Canterbury in 1556. Thought to be harsh, the level of Pole's involvement in the Marian Persecutions is disputed, but some now believe that he was inclined to leniency. He died on November 17, 1558, the same day as Mary I, during an influenza epidemic.

PHILIP II OF SPAIN

ON MARY'S DEATH, Philip proposed a union between himself and Elizabeth I, only to be rebuffed by the Protestant Virgin Queen. He later showed his displeasure when he sent the full might of the Spanish Armada against England under her rule (although this was to fail spectacularly).

Philip was a man of such contrasts—pious and deeply Catholic on the one hand, but capable of being cruel and unscrupulous, especially to Protestants. Hated by the English, he was loved and respected by his own countrymen and women, bringing great riches to his beloved Spain.

> Cranmer denied his earlier recantations … plunging the hand that had signed his recantations into the fire to punish it.

recantation and the law of reprieve that should have been granted to Cranmer, Mary allowed him the chance to make a further, public recantation prior to his execution. However, by this stage he may have believed his death to be inevitable. Cranmer denied his earlier recantations and proclaimed himself a true believer of the Protestant faith, plunging the hand that had signed his recantations into the fire to punish it. The man who wrote The Book of Common Prayer and largely shaped Anglican religion for hundreds of years was duly burned at the stake for his treason and previous crimes, dying a martyr.

But Mary was far from finished. Her aim was to stamp out Protestantism and heresy at any cost, restoring her country to its previous greatness.

Union with Spain

Shortly after her accession, Mary—eager to secure her line with male heirs—started looking around for a husband. This time she was able to make up her own mind. Whoever he was, he had to be Catholic.

Now 37 years old, Mary looked at potential suitors from England, such as Edward Courtenay, a favorite of

Mary's whom she made Earl of Devon, and Reginald Pole, the son of Mary's old governess who had always supported her mothers' marriage to Henry. (Pole would become a staunch ally of Mary's but her own laws on marrying clergymen put paid to any unlikely union between the two.) However, in her eagerness

Below: However much Mary believed herself to be in love, her choice of marriage to Philip was political and proof of her commitment to a Catholic country. Unfortunately, many of her subjects did not appreciate the idea of a foreigner on the English throne.

Opposite: This portrait of Philip II was painted by the Italian painter Tiziano Vecellio, better known as Titian. Titian painted many works for Philip II, including this portrait, which was sent to Mary after she expressed interest in fulfilling Charles V's desire for the union.

Above: Philip II, King of Spain, receives the rulership of the Netherlands from his father Emperor Charles V, in 1556.

> To put Philip on equal footing with his bride, Charles presented him with the Kingdoms of Naples and Jerusalem.

to reunite the Church of England with Rome, Mary sought the advice of Charles V, whom she had once said could choose a husband for her. Unsurprisingly, Charles chose his only son, Philip II of Spain.

Philip was in line to inherit his father's vast empire on his death and he was a devout Catholic. To put Philip on equal footing with his bride, Charles presented him with the Kingdoms of Naples and Jerusalem. In principle, the union was a good one. However, Philip was ten years younger than his bride

Opposite: This picture shows the rack: a typical medieval torture device used for extracting information. Unfortunate victims were strapped on by their wrists and ankles, then a handle was turned that stretched the victim's whole body, causing excruciating pain.

and viewed the union as purely political. There was also huge outcry from the English council, who were appalled at the thought of a foreigner becoming King. As a man, Philip could take over rule of England on Mary's death. This was unthinkable.

Unfortunately, Mary would not be moved. She had made her decision, based in part on a portrait of Philip by Titian that had been sent to her. Girlishly imagining herself in love, Mary was delighted with her husband-to-be, although it is thought that Philip was not so happy when he first saw her in the flesh! She was also happy to make a union with Spain, her beloved mother's country. A compromise took place, meaning that Philip was King for the duration of the marriage only. He was unable to make any proclamation or sign any treaty on his own—possibly a sensible rule, as Philip spoke no English—and he needed his wife to co-rule with him on every detail and could not appoint any foreigners to the English council. Another stipulation was that England was under no obligation

> Edward Courtenay, Mary's potential suitor … expected her to marry him, but he quickly turned his affections towards Elizabeth …

to support Spain in acts of war. Philip was allowed the concession of it being treason for anyone to deny his authority. He reluctantly agreed to the marriage treaty and the couple wed on July 25, 1554.

Wyatt Rebellion

One of the most significant outcomes of Mary's proposed union was the passionate public outcry. Led largely by Protestants, a rebellion broke out in March 1554 that called for Mary to marry an Englishman. While the reasons given were mainly political, with subjects wanting to hold on to their sovereignty and not let it fall into the hands of foreign powers, Mary also suffered a backlash against her strict religious reforms. A plot developed in which the rebels would converge on London. If Mary insisted on marrying Philip she would be replaced by Elizabeth, who would then marry Edward Courtenay in Mary's place.

Led by Thomas Wyatt, James Croft, Peter Carew and Henry Grey (Jane Grey's father)—all influential landowners—the original intent was to gather forces from around the country and lead an organized attack on London on March 18. Edward Courtenay, Mary's potential suitor, showed his true colors by encouraging the rebellion with no thought to the consequences for Mary. It may be that he truly cared for Mary and expected her to marry him, but he quickly turned his affections towards Elizabeth when it became apparent that Mary had no intention of doing so. Courtenay was exiled soon after the rebellion, losing the chance to wed either sister.

The whole rebellion started to unravel when a plot was suspected. Simon Renard, the Spanish ambassador and Bishop Gardiner joined forces to protect the Queen. Courtenay was arrested and revealed everything. Refusing to back down, the date for the attack was brought forward and Wyatt managed to raise a substantial force, occupying the town of Rochester. Troops were sent to disperse the rebellion, but the Queen's potential marriage had become so

unpopular that many soldiers joined the rebels, who now numbered upwards of 4000 men. With tension mounting, Mary agreed to hear Wyatt's demands. It was here that the overconfident Wyatt lost support. Instead of voicing his original fears about Mary's marriage to Philip, Wyatt demanded that she surrender the Tower of London to him and place herself under his control. Mary quickly followed up with her famous speech at the Guildhall, which secured her much sympathy and support.

Mary had the charisma and charm of her bluff, hearty father. Her speech cleverly combined this with vulnerability, turning her gender into a positive aspect. Queen Mary assured her people of her deep love for them and promised that she would seek advice on her marriage, following whatever course was best for the country. The Queen's stirring speech remains emotional:

By their answers, the marriage is found to be the least of their quarrel; for, swerving from their former demands, they now arrogantly requite the GOVERNANCE OF OUR PERSON, the KEEPING OF OUR TOWN, and the PLACING OF OUR COUNCILLORS. What I am, loving subjects, yet know your Queen, to whom, at my coronation, ye promised allegiance and obedience, I was then wedded to the realm, and to the laws of the same, the spousal ring whereof I wear here on my finger, and it never has and never shall be left off.

I cannot tell you how naturally a mother loveth her children, for I never had any, but if the subjects may be loved as a mother doth her child, then assure yourselves that I, your sovereign lady and your Queen, do earnestly love and favor you. I cannot but think you love me in return; and thus, bound in concord, we shall be able I doubt not, to give these rebels a speedy overthrow.

I am neither so desirous of wedding, nor so precisely wedded to my will, that I needs must have a husband. Hitherto I have lived a virgin, and I doubt not, with God's grace, to live still. But if, as my ancestors have done, it might please God that I should leave you a SUCCESSOR to be your GOVERNOR, I trust you would rejoice thereat; also; I know it would be to your comfort. Yet, if I thought this marriage would endanger any of you, my loving subjects, or the royal estate of this English realm, I would never consent thereto nor marry while I lived. On the word of a Queen I assure you, that if the marriage appear not before the court of Parliament, nobility and commons, for the singular benefit of the whole realm, then will abstain not only from this, but from any other.

THOMAS WYATT THE YOUNGER

Thomas Wyatt the Younger (named so to distinguish him from his father, Sir Thomas Wyatt, the poet and one of Henry VII's ambassadors) was a Catholic, but his experience of viewing the Spanish Inquisition as a youngster had left a powerful mark on him. He became staunchly anti-Spanish and was utterly opposed to Mary's foreign marriage. Wyatt was supported by other nobles, gathering many followers. However, he lost ground when he arrogantly demanded that Mary should place herself under his control. He was also a previous suitor of Anne Boleyn before her ill-fated marriage.

Painted by Sarah, Countess of Essex in 1825, this portrait depicts Sir Thomas Wyatt the Younger in a classical style, perhaps to emphasise the heroic nature of his rebellion.

Above: Thomas Wyatt was executed for treason on April 11, 1554. The executioner is pictured holding up Wyatt's head for the gathered crowds to see. Wyatt's head was later displayed in a gallows at Hay Hill near Hyde Park in London, before being stolen on April 17.

While Wyatt did make it to Southwark in February 1554, the city of London remained closed to the rebels, held fast by Mary's supporters. Some supporters reached the outskirts of London, but the overwhelming might of the Queen's army broke up the rebellion. Wyatt later surrendered and was executed along with around 90 rebels. Mary was willing to forgive to a certain extent—she pardoned many of the remaining rebels—but an example had to be made to prove she was not weak. Consequently, Lady Jane Grey and her husband were also executed along with her father Henry.

But there was one person whose involvement could have led to execution. Elizabeth would have benefited on the success of the rebellion by becoming

> Mary had to tread very carefully. She was already suspicious … and annoyed that Elizabeth would not accept Catholicism herself.

Queen. Here, Mary had to tread very carefully. She was already suspicious of her sister and annoyed that Elizabeth would not accept Catholicism herself. Now, additional suspicion of her involvement with the rebel's plot led to Elizabeth being imprisoned in the Tower and interrogated. Elizabeth denied any involvement or knowledge of the plots and there was no proof to contradict her statements. With no grounds to press for treason, but still wary of her sister, Mary had Elizabeth placed under house arrest at Woodstock Palace, where she remained for almost a year.

Turmoil and Misfortune

Mary went ahead with her marriage to Philip under the conditions attached by the Privy Council, meaning that England was safe from falling into the hands of the Spanish. Mary had gained the husband and union with Spain she so desired, but the recent rebellion was a taste of things to come.

Mary's religious policy continued. Heresy laws were reinstated, which led to the brutal and hugely unpopular Marian Persecutions. This alone would have been enough to diminish support for the Queen. In addition to other unfortunate events, Mary quickly became uniformly feared and reviled.

Home and Away

Most of Ireland was still under English rule, although there had been rumblings of discontent for decades. Mary tried to quell any further rebellions by settling English colonists throughout the Midlands to reduce these attacks. Ireland would continue to threaten English peace well into Elizabeth's reign.

Philip had long tried to convince Mary to support Spain in a war with France. While under no obligation to do so under the terms of their marriage treaty, various French plots to depose Mary meant that in 1557, war was declared with France. This led to strained relations with the papacy, as Pope Paul IV was an ally of France. Things got far worse when the French took back Calais in January 1558. This was a huge loss of prestige for England, who had managed to keep this toehold in France for over two centuries. The war was also costly at a time when the

country needed every penny it could spare. Mary was to shoulder the blame and humiliation as the war was seen as a result of her marriage to Philip.

Life at home was hard under Mary. While much of this was nothing to do with her decisions, it nevertheless made things uncomfortable. Heavy rains meant that floods ruined harvest after harvest. Food was scarce and famines were becoming all the more common. Trade was low, especially with cloth, and the Spanish trade routes had tied up many other opportunities. Mary tried hard to counteract the debasement of the pound that had started under Henry VIII, but her rule was not long enough to see any benefit from this. She also sought to open up new trade routes and commercial prospects, with seafaring adventurers seeking links for trade. Had she ruled for longer than five years, the tide might have turned and England may have started to see a profit. As it was, by early 1558 things looked bleak for Mary and for England.

Right: Despite Mary's impassioned speech to her public in February 1554, when she promised never to marry anyone that her subjects did not approve of, Mary and Philip can be seen here entering London later that same year.

> Mary truly believed it was her duty to stamp out sacrilege and stop heretics corrupting and damning others.

Marian Persecutions

These early executions led to a wide-scale persecution of Protestants, numbering between 280 to 300 people. While Mary actually put to death a mere fraction of those her father executed, her reputation as a destructive force, hell-bent on cutting out anyone she saw as a canker, is well known. However, Mary truly believed it was her duty to stamp out sacrilege and stop heretics corrupting and damning others.

Beginning with the newly reinstated heresy laws, from January 20, 1555 it was legal to punish anyone found guilty of heresy against the Catholic Church. Now sanctioned by Parliament, Mary's council sought to show their support for the traditional faith by purging the land of heretics. With some members more proactive than others, the more orthodox and conservative council members such as Bishop Gardiner and Edmund Bonner, the Bishop of London, made examples of prominent, well-known people. Bonner especially became widely detested for his part in the persecutions, dubbed "Bloody" Bonner by his enemies. Almost all of the victims were burned at the stake, including nobles, Church leaders, men, women and even a few children. There were no political motives here, as is often the case with executions. It was purely about religious persecution.

The medieval method of burning heretics at the stake was such a savage death that it angered many. Mary and her agents of death were also taking away much-

> The medieval method of burning heretics at the stake was such a savage death that it angered many. … taking away much-loved churchmen who were known to be pious, loyal and charitable.

Above: Philip's forces beat the French in Picardy in the Battle of Saint Quentin. Mary sent English troops to support the Spanish, even though this went against the terms of her marriage treaty.

loved churchmen who were known to be pious, loyal and charitable. The persecutions had the opposite effect than they were meant to have. Mary truly thought that by sacrificing a few bodies to the flames on earth, she would be saving countless souls from the fires of hell. But her sacrifice of the Englishmen and women she professed to love so much left her universally hated and many people turning to Protestantism in response to the horrific burnings done in the name of Catholicism. Now

dubbed the Marian Martyrs, the first man executed was John Rogers, a clergyman at St Paul's Cathedral, on February 4, 1555. The final recorded burnings occurred just days before Mary's death on November 17, 1558 and would have continued if she had not died.

It could be said that Mary felt the high price of lives was worth paying if it meant that the majority of English souls would be saved. Unfortunately, the persecutions backfired badly. Watching martyrs burn for their faith caused a Protestant backlash that could not be controlled. By the time of Mary's death, the prisons were bursting with believers who refused to renounce their faith. Mary had failed.

Mary: The Woman

Mary had long been eager to have children, both to secure the legacy of her throne and for Philip and her to become parents. In September 1554, only two months after their marriage, Mary began exhibiting signs of being with child. Soon the whole court believed her to be carrying a child. Her periods stopped, she put on weight and experienced nausea in the mornings. Unwisely, Mary even let the gathered crowds see her bump during a public appearance. Soon the whole country knew that a royal baby was on its way. Celebrations took place and plans were made. At the age of 38, with health problems behind her, no

… Mary's enlarged abdomen began to recede. There were no signs of a child ever having been present. Mary was devastated …

chances could be taken. If Mary died in childbirth, Philip was to be made Regent of their child.

Towards the end of the pregnancy, Elizabeth was reconciled to her sister and returned to court to witness the birth, which was expected around May of 1555. However, the months passed and there was no sign of a child. Rumors spread around the court that Mary was not actually pregnant. These were quashed, but in July 1555, Mary's enlarged abdomen began to recede. There were no signs of a child ever having been present. Mary was devastated and her reputation was damaged further. Her belief may have come from the idea that God would grant them children who would continue her work in His name, despite her advancing years.

Philip soon left England for Flanders, where he waged war against France. Mary was left to face her country alone. The depression that had dogged her younger years returned and she could not be consoled.

BURNED AT THE STAKE

POSSIBLY FOLLOWING THE example of the Spanish Inquisition (which dispatched 2,000 people using this technique), the method of execution for heretics was death by burning.

This was no clean, quick death like beheading. Being burned at the stake could take hours, leaving the unfortunate victim suffering intense agony. A tall metal stake would be placed in the ground, to which the victim would be chained. Some sort of flammable material would be packed around the stake, then set alight. Resin or pitch would often be poured over the victim to encourage the burning. There was a risk of the victim dying from shock or carbon monoxide poisoning before they burned to death. These were the lucky ones. If the fire was smaller, it would first burn the legs and arms before travelling up the torso, chest and head.

Below: The Burning of ten protestant martyrs in Lewes, Sussex, 1557. The victims depicted are Richard Woodman, George Stevens, Alexander Hosman, William Mainard, Thomasina Wood, Margery Morris, James Morris, Denis Burges, Ann Ashton and Mary Groves.

HERE LIES MARY

WESTMINSTER ABBEY HOLDS the spectacular Lady Chapel, build by Henry VII for his family. As well as his wife, mother and his own tombs, it holds the tomb of Elizabeth and Mary, two sisters united in death. Mary was interred in December 1558. For a long time her remains lay under a pile of smashed altar stones. On Elizabeth I's death, James I (her successor) built a magnificent tomb for both sisters to rest together. It is striking that only Elizabeth's image is depicted on the tomb. Mary, in death as in life, was pushed aside in favor of her more celebrated relatives.

She also feared that her false pregnancy had been God's punishment for her "lenient" treatment of heretics. The Queen whom everyone had such confidence in was now a damaged woman, Mary never having found it easy to reconcile being a good wife with her role as supreme ruler (an issue Elizabeth, with all of her mother's sexuality and craftiness, would not suffer from).

> It is possible that her phantom pregnancies and abdominal swelling were caused by ovarian cancer ... Mary was now sure she was with child and amended her will to take her issue into account.

Shortly before her death in November, Mary again thought herself to be pregnant. She was now 42 years old and nearing the end of her life. It is possible that her phantom pregnancies and abdominal swelling were caused by ovarian cancer, which may have eventually killed her had she not contracted influenza. However, Mary was now sure she was with child and amended her will to take her issue into account. When this second pregnancy came to nothing, this was amended once more to include a codicil naming her "next heir and successor" following Henry VIII's will. It is thought that she couldn't bring herself to name Elizabeth as her successor in writing. Mary pleaded with Elizabeth to uphold the Catholic faith she had reintroduced during her violent reign. She died knowing that the likelihood of everything she had worked for would come to nothing. Mary had faced rejection from first her father, then her brother. Her husband was abroad—as he had been for most of their marriage—and she left no child to carry on the legacy. Is it any wonder that she turned to God?

"Queen ... and by the same title a King"
The many issues that combined under Mary's have led to her five years as Queen of England to be seen as a failure, a waste of time and life. England was no better off because of Mary. In fact many were worse off. Those who had fled or suffered during the persecutions and rebellions; those whose livelihood had suffered and those who had once again been affected by about-turns in religious doctrine were all united in welcoming Elizabeth. Crowds cheered at Mary's death and welcomed the accession of Elizabeth. The realm was eager to put the horrors of the last few years behind them and embrace a monarch who would be more tolerant of the needs of her people.

For a long time, Mary's unpopular decisions were highlighted, as well as the futility of the persecutions in her name. From around the seventeenth century she was abhorred as Bloody Mary and blamed for everything that had gone wrong in England during her reign, including the bad weather and famines that actually begun under Edward's reign. Heralded as proof of her failures were the Persecutions, the loss of Calais and her lack of heir. With Protestantism gaining in popularity, she became a figurehead of the corruption of the Catholic Church. John Foxe's *Book*

Opposite: The tomb of Mary and Elizabeth in Westminster Abbey bears a Latin inscription that reads: "Consorts in realm and tomb, here we sleep, Elizabeth and Mary, sisters, in hope of resurrection."

of Martyrs, which recorded every person to be executed under the Marian Persecutions, would become the most widely read book in England after the Bible. The graphic illustrations depicting such gruesome events still send a chill down the spine. Her acts may well have caused many to turn away from Catholicism in disgust. Certainly after her reign there was more indifference, perhaps due to so many years of religious discord.

There is the argument that Mary just didn't have enough time to implement the good policies she introduced—which included halting the debasement of the currency, and naval expansion and exploration

Her acts may well have caused many to turn away from Catholicism in disgust.

that continued under Elizabeth—but who knows how far Bloody Mary would have taken the religious persecutions? Mary's time of tyranny was over and she had left a country in turmoil, eager for stability and peace.

Opposite: This portrait of Mary I in later life shows a saddened woman whose childless condition weighed on her mind. Mary lived in hope of a child right up to 1558, the final year of her life. Now widely reviled, the death of the first Queen of England would be celebrated.

Below: A mother and her two daughters burned for heresy in 1556, became known as the Guernsey Martyrs. One daughter was heavily pregnant and her baby burst forth into the fire. Foxe records that the attending bailiff ordered the baby to be burned with its mother.

The Burning of Katherine Cawches, and her two Daughters in the Isle of Garnsey.

VI

ELIZABETH:
CULT OF THE VIRGIN QUEEN

Henry VIII,
King of England
b. 1491–d. 1547

Anne Boleyn
b. 1501–d. 1536
m. 1533

Elizabeth I
b. 1533–d. 1603

Overshadowing every Tudor monarch—save perhaps her flagrantly infamous father—Elizabeth I elevated herself above the mistakes of her siblings to achieve venerated status, which saw advances in culture and overseas trade, the end of decades of religious turmoil and the crushing defeat of the Spanish Armada. Becoming so notorious for refusing to marry that her Virgin Queen status created cults and legends, Elizabeth I both inspired and infuriated—but she always did it her way.

"I will have but one mistress and no master."—ELIZABETH I

B orn in 1533, shortly after Anne Boleyn, her mother, had married Henry VIII and caused him to break with the Catholic Church, Elizabeth would spend her entire childhood in a reforming country with all the confusion and unrest that comes with it. With Anne Boleyn executed before

Opposite" Princess Elizabeth is shown here looking every inch the future monarch. While she was of more use to her family as a potential political alliance through matrimony, Elizabeth I would never condone a marriage that gave anyone power over her country and person.

Elizabeth's third birthday—leaving the young princess discarded and removed from succession—the shadow of bad blood hung over Elizabeth for many years. Nevertheless, any child of Henry VIII's was due a certain level of care and Elizabeth (as well as her sister Mary) would find herself in and out of favor depending on Henry's mood and marital status. Useful in forming alliances with foreign countries, Elizabeth was a highly prized potential wife, so she had to be well educated and able to act like the princess she believed herself to be.

Elizabeth's education was first-rate and she excelled at languages. Intelligent, articulate and open-minded, by a combination of her schooling and family circumstances, Elizabeth grew up quickly.

Her maturation would take a darker turn when her brother, Edward VI, became King of England in 1547. Catherine Parr, Henry's widow, married Thomas Seymour soon after Henry's death. Elizabeth—now reinstated as Edward's successor under the terms of Henry's will—was under the care of Catherine Parr and living in her household. It was here that Elizabeth first attracted male attention.

Elizabeth was sent away in May 1548, and she soon had her own household and trusted attendants.

Thomas Seymour, whose brother Edward was Lord Protector of England during Edward's minority, engaged in inappropriate behavior with his wife's stepdaughter. Thomas was an attractive man in his late thirties at this stage. He was angry at being unable to secure the powerful position awarded his brother and sought to gain control in a much more underhanded and ominous way. Thomas engaged in horseplay with the teenage princess, entering her room at night and tickling and embracing her.

When Catherine Parr first discovered this, Thomas used his hold over his wife to assure her that the games were innocent. Catherine even joined in occasionally, holding the girl down while Thomas tickled or teased her. Perhaps Catherine thought that her presence would curtail the activities from going any further than they should. It was only when Catherine found the two alone together in an embrace that she put a stop to things. Elizabeth was sent away in May 1548, and she soon had her own household and trusted attendants.

Now safe from Thomas' attentions, Elizabeth was able to put these unsavory events behind her for a short time. However, after Catherine Parr's death in September 1548, Thomas Seymour tried to renew his relationship with Elizabeth, this time needing no

Below: Elizabeth wrote many letters to her step-mother Catherine Parr, with whom she remained close after her removal from the household. It was Catherine who advised Elizabeth to guard her actions as she may one day be Queen, advice that Elizabeth would follow closely.

Right: After marrying Catherine Parr, Henry VIII's widow and one of the wealthiest women in England, Thomas Seymour was prepared to seduce his step-daughter in order to marry a potential Queen! When this failed, Thomas sought power by manipulating Edward VI.

subterfuge. He sought to marry the princess and secure his authority. Thomas was also working to undermine his brother's position of power over Edward VI. Then nearly 11 years old, Edward was regularly visited by Thomas, who gave him gifts of money and dripped poison in his ear, subtly suggesting that Edward Seymour was usurping the young King's authority. This combination of deceit was to be his undoing. Thomas was arrested in 1549, his attentions towards Elizabeth and plots to overthrow his brother leading to his execution that same year.

Lust for Power

A seductive and charismatic man, it was only when Thomas' jealousy and lust for power became too overt that he ended up destroying himself. An interesting note is that when Elizabeth was interrogated to build a case against the would-be usurper, she refused to say anything that might incriminate Thomas (her own self-preservation instincts were learned early). While her silence was not enough to save Thomas, the whole experience affected Elizabeth and may have influenced her decision never to marry. The idea that she may have been privy to Thomas' intentions to marry her and ensure she became Queen over her brother and sister is unsubstantiated but intriguing, as is the level of power Elizabeth would have awarded Thomas were this to happen.

... by the age of 15 she had seen and experienced enough damaging relationships ...

All in all, Elizabeth had to mature quickly and, by the age of 15 she had seen and experienced enough damaging relationships to remain circumspect with her reputation. This dangerous brush with treason would not be her last and even Elizabeth's excellent skills of talking herself out of trouble would soon be tested to their limits.

THE VIRGIN QUEEN

HAVING SEEN FOR herself how destructive marriage could be (with her own mother executed before Elizabeth's third birthday), Elizabeth was in no hurry to wed. Add to this her sister Mary's ill-advised foreign union, phantom pregnancies and lovelorn misery, plus the fact that any man the Queen married would be in a position of authority at least equal to her, meant that Elizabeth was understandably cagey when it came to making such a commitment. Whatever her reasons, the Virgin Queen status saw Elizabeth idolized as an icon or even a goddess, which she herself cultivated and encouraged. This status raised her above most people and was part of the legend that became Gloriana.

Below: "Princess Elizabeth at the Tower" (oil on canvas) by artist Robert Alexander Hillingford (1825–1904).

A King's Sister

As Edward VI's sister, Elizabeth caused little trouble, especially compared to Mary who openly flouted the King's orders by having Catholic masses said in Latin, to which she invited all and sundry. The siblings were close when they were children, but their father's various intrigues meant that the shadow of suspicion would always blight the family. No one was completely secure on the throne while the others were part of the family, no matter what precautions were set down. This would be demonstrated after Edward's death. It was when Edward was very ill in 1553 that he chose to go against the wishes of Henry VIII and disinherit both his sisters. Edward's main issue was with Mary, whose Catholic beliefs meant that all Edward's attempts in forming a secure Protestant religion in England would come to nothing. But in order to disinherit Mary, Edward would also have to disinherit Elizabeth. This he did in favor of Lady Jane Grey. Jane's infamous nine-day rule gave Elizabeth another glimpse at how tenuous the life of a monarch could be, and she learned just how dangerous being named as a successor could be.

> It was when Edward was very ill in 1553 that he chose to go against the wishes of Henry VIII and disinherit both his sisters … in favor of Lady Jane Grey.

A Queen's Sister

With Edward dead, Mary quickly took the throne to avid public support. Life changed dramatically once again for Elizabeth, now living at court with her sister. Mary's position was secure at first, with her decision to reinstate the Catholic faith initially popular. However, the rapid alteration yet again—this time from a reformed Protestant faith back to traditional Catholicism—was too much for many. Rumblings grew to rebellion and in 1554 Thomas Wyatt led a revolt against Mary. Their initial aim was to avoid a union with Spain and a potential foreign King. But things quickly spiralled. Elizabeth became a figurehead of reason and enlightenment, in stark comparison to the tyrannical, irrational Bloody Mary. A new plot arose, by which Mary would be deposed in favor of Elizabeth, who would then marry Edward Courtenay, a previous suitor.

With the rebellion quashed, Elizabeth again became the focus of interrogation. The roots of Mary's distrust perhaps lay in deep affection for her mother, who was so viciously pushed aside by Anne Boleyn, Elizabeth's mother. Mary also found it hard to forget how Anne had favored her beloved Elizabeth, the result of which saw Mary tossed aside by her father. Mary's suspicions were deep-rooted, despite there being no proof that Elizabeth had taken any part in the rebellion or had even been aware of Courtenay's plans. On March 18, 1554, Elizabeth was taken to the Tower of London, where she would remain for two months. Only when she had been repeatedly interrogated and questioned— during which time she never wavered from the protestations of innocence and love for her sister—did Elizabeth leave her prison for Woodstock, where she was placed under house arrest for nearly a year.

Support for Elizabeth flourished during this time, as Mary's religious intolerance grew and grew. Elizabeth may well have remained under house arrest until Mary came up with a way to remove the threat she posed, had it not been for Mary's pregnancy in 1555. Practicalities had to be dealt with, even if personal opinion was clouded. If Mary had a healthy child, Elizabeth was unlikely to ever become Queen. However, the precarious nature of childhood meant that Mary needed to have her sister in place for the succession if she were to die in childbirth. In the end, the plans were unnecessary. Mary would never carry a child to term, her only pregnancies being figments of her damaged imagination.

Mary's health declined and, on November 17, 1558, she died leaving Elizabeth as her heir under the terms of Henry VIII's original will.

Under Elizabeth, the Tudor line would continue for nearly 45 years. She had learned much from her parents, brother and sister. From her father she acquired the right to rule above all her subjects and the charisma to do so successfully. Her mother's memory embedded Elizabeth with a caution that meant she rarely made rash decisions. Having seen how religious swings could result in rebellion, these were treated with moderation. Keeping her public as well as powerful allies on side would be a challenge, but Elizabeth had

already escaped two charges of treason and was more than capable of using her skills of manipulation when necessary. At the age of 25, with the blood of her parents coursing through her veins and the mistakes of her siblings as stepping stones, Elizabeth I would shape her image into one that inspired an almost cult-like following.

Becoming Elizabeth I

While there were issues with Elizabeth becoming ruler—namely her being a woman and not sticking to the Catholic faith that Mary had reintroduced— by and large the country was happy that Elizabeth was to become Queen. Her coronation took place on January 15, 1559 and was met with cheers, dancing, music and celebrations, the dark days of Bloody Mary's reign quickly fading in the brilliance of the dazzling young Queen.

Elizabeth assured her council that she would heed their advice and look to them and her people for

Above: This striking illustration shows Elizabeth on her coronation procession along the River Thames in London. Already the Queen had proven that she needed no one to help put her on the throne.

guidance. She sought to reduce religious turmoil by uniting the country under a Protestant religion with elements of traditional Catholicism still present, not making the same mistakes as her siblings in pushing reforms too far, too fast. While this decision was generally well received in England, it left the realm open to attack from traditional Catholic countries, which might be tempted to try their luck against a heretical England. As Elizabeth seems to have been so flexible in her religious beliefs, a strong argument in favor of Protestantism was her illegitimacy in the eyes of the Catholic faith, the marriage between her parents

Opposite: Elizabeth is pictured here in her coronation robes, which bear a pattern of Tudor roses. Her hair is loose in the traditional style for a Queen on her coronation, which also highlights her innocence.

LOYAL SECRETARY: WILLIAM CECIL, BARON BURGHLEY

WILLIAM CECIL HAD successfully navigated his way through English Parliament under Henry VIII, Edward VI and Mary I, despite occasionally falling from grace. Ever loyal to Tudor monarchs, Cecil became Elizabeth's secretary soon after her accession. He was a master of diplomacy and could take a hard line. Cecil enforced some decisions that Elizabeth was unsure about, including the execution of Mary, Queen of Scots. A constant support to his Queen throughout his life, Cecil's politics on Elizabeth's behalf saw the creation of an intelligence service and the beginning of financial security for the crown. His son, Robert, would later act for Elizabeth in a similar capacity and two of Cecil's descendants became British Prime Ministers.

not being seen as valid by the Catholic Church. If she had chosen Catholicism, Elizabeth would have left herself open to opposition from legitimate heirs to the throne, such as Mary, Queen of Scots. This would still be an obstacle for Elizabeth later in her reign.

Elizabeth took the popular route of renouncing the Heresy laws, under which so much harm had been done in Mary's name. She did pass the Act of Uniformity in 1559, making it mandatory to attend church and follow the Book of Common Prayer, but sanctions for not doing so were far less severe than under Edward or Mary's reign. Elizabeth became Supreme Governor of the Church of England (it was a step too far to make a woman Head of the Church, no matter who she was) and a new Act of Supremacy was passed on 8 May to this effect.

> Elizabeth took the popular route of renouncing the Heresy laws, under which so much harm had been done …

With the Queen of childbearing and marriageable age, there was soon huge debate over who would become Elizabeth's husband. But here, Elizabeth would follow her own heart and spend the next 25 years toying with her council and many potential suitors.

"Rather a Beggar and Single than a Queen and Married"

Elizabeth's attitude to marriage has been well documented and is a constant source of fascination. Having seen the destructive nature of love in her parents' relationship as well as the political consequences of her sister's marriage, it is no wonder that Elizabeth was wary when it came to taking a husband. What is more surprising is her lack of interest in securing the Tudor line with her own descendants.

There are many explanations as to why Elizabeth never bent to the council's often overwhelming influence and also why she never married to secure the Tudor line through her heirs. Some suggest a physical reason, such as infertility. Elizabeth herself made reference to this when she referred to herself as

Above: This dramatic illustration shows the death of Amy Robsart, Robert Dudley's wife. Dudley would certainly have a lot to gain from being able to marry Elizabeth, but the Queen was not prepared to have her reputation sullied or her position usurped by a man.

"barren stock" after hearing that Mary, Queen of Scots gave birth to her son James. Others look to her early relationship with the sinister Seymour, which put her off men. In Elizabeth's own words, she intended to be married to her country and live by her motto *semper eadem* ("always the same"). The queen of beguilement then used her virginity as an extremely clever propaganda tool to elevate herself above her equals. On the other hand, Elizabeth was notoriously bad at making her mind up! Perhaps she just couldn't make a decision.

While Elizabeth seemed determined never to marry, she did have a number of suitors, some of whom she encouraged and even seemed to care for deeply. The intrigue surrounding her private life remains to this day, as ever more films and books devoted to the subject appear. This intelligent, striking, vulnerable yet powerful young woman who controlled a kingdom attracted much attention and remains an enigma to this day.

> On September 8, Amy was found dead in her home, lying at the bottom of a flight of stairs with her neck snapped.

Dudley: The Constant Favorite

One man stands head and shoulders above the others as Elizabeth's potential husband. Robert Dudley had been a friend of the Queen's since childhood. He lost his favored family position due to his father, John Dudley's, actions in supporting Lady Jane Grey as monarch after Edward. The entire Dudley family fell under suspicion and Robert spent time in the Tower of London. Under Elizabeth, Dudley became Master of the Horse in 1558, then a member of her Privy Council and Lord Steward of the household soon after. Dudley was always a favorite of the Queen's. A married man, it was long suspected that he would marry Elizabeth on the death of his wife, Amy. Amy had been ill for some time, meaning that she did not live at court with her husband. This made it easier for Dudley and Elizabeth to form an attachment. Had Amy died naturally of her illness, who knows how their relationship might have progressed? However, Amy was to die under far more suspicious circumstances.

Rumors of an attachment between the married Dudley and the unmarried Queen were rife at court, especially as Elizabeth refused several other marriage proposals. It was in 1560 that these rumors turned ugly. On September 8, Amy was found dead in her home, lying at the bottom of a flight of stairs with her neck snapped.

It was the day of a local fair and Amy had insisted that all of her servants be away from the household. Dudley was at Windsor Castle with Elizabeth at the time, so direct suspicion of involvement could not be levied against him. An investigation was carried out, which found the cause of death to be accidental; however, Dudley had caused many to turn against him by his conceit and lack of scruples. William Cecil—whom Dudley was desperate to get rid of—spread rumors of a plot to poison Amy and the gossip was spread gleefully by Dudley's many enemies. While Elizabeth supported her lover, such was the controversy that she would have been risking mass rebellion if she had then wed Dudley. Having seen where such folly and misery led her sister, Elizabeth was not prepared to risk her reign, even for the man she loved.

> … the knowledge of her worsening health could have prompted a frightened, miserable woman to take desperate action.

It is impossible to say whether Amy's cause of death was malicious. Perhaps Amy had wanted it to look deliberately suspicious, trying to land doubt and accusation on her unfaithful husband. Equally, the knowledge of her worsening health could have prompted a frightened, miserable woman to take desperate action. The scandal her death caused meant that Dudley could never marry Elizabeth.

Dudley remained unmarried for 18 years after his wife's death. He refused to wed Mary, Queen of Scots, even though she agreed to the proposal, believing it was the only way she would succeed Elizabeth. When he did remarry, Elizabeth was still jealous enough to ban his new wife, Lettice Knollys, from court. Despite these intrigues, they remained close friends until his death in 1588. Many believed that if Elizabeth ever did take a husband, it would have been Robert. But their love was never to be.

His personal relationship with Elizabeth overshadowing his political career, Dudley was one of the council who implemented the execution of Mary, Queen of Scots, which Elizabeth was reluctant to do. Dudley was also a confirmed patron of the arts, being one of the founders of the original Oxford University Press. He had his own company of players and supported Edmund Spenser in writing his poetry.

ROBERT DUDLEY

DUDLEY AND ELIZABETH had their ups and downs, but they remained loyal to each other and in many respects acted like a married couple. She was deeply hurt when he married another woman, yet he proved his undying loyalty to Elizabeth many times over.

It was Dudley who led her horse during the mesmerizing speech at Tilbury, when the warrior Queen donned armor and met her forces in the midst of the Spanish Armada.

On his death, Elizabeth is thought to have locked herself inside her rooms for days. His final letter to her was found in her personal possessions after her death 15 years later.

Left: Mary, Queen of Scots, is pictured here with her husband, Francis II of France. They were married for less than three years before Francis' death in December 1560.

Quarrels with Scotland

With no surviving (legitimate) siblings, Elizabeth still had to fear the usurpation of her crown. Her relative, Mary, Queen of Scots, held the Scottish throne and fears were rife that the French would invade England through Scotland, using the auld alliance to finally bring an end to warring and reinstate a Catholic ruler in England. Mary, who had married Francis II of France in 1558 after spending most of her life in the French court, returned to Scotland in 1561 as Queen Regnant.

To avoid any demands on her throne, Elizabeth tried to force a union between Mary and Robert Dudley. Through this marriage, Elizabeth envisaged that she would be able to keep a close eye on Mary and avoid war with Scotland. However, this union did not go ahead. Mary was also cause for concern as she refused to ratify a treaty put in place to avoid war with France. She was not a fan of the Protestant church that had been established

Elizabeth would discard many more suitors during her reign, as well as pick her favorites from the most dashing, alluring and intriguing men of her court. Equally generous and forgiving, or ruthless and discriminating, Elizabeth revelled in their chivalric attentions while remaining aloof. As always, the Virgin Queen used her feminine wiles and sexuality to get exactly what she wanted. Her additional power as sovereign meant she could easily rid herself of bothersome men when they bored her.

Mary, Queen of Scots, held the Scottish throne and fears were rife that the French would invade England through Scotland, using the auld alliance to … reinstate a Catholic ruler in England.

GOLF: THE SPORT OF QUEENS

MARY WAS KNOWN for her love of golf, being one of the first women in Scotland to take up and regularly play the sport. She learned the game during her childhood at the French court and continued to play when she returned to Scotland. While this healthy outdoor pursuit was acceptable for a Queen, Mary was slated for enjoying a game only days after the vicious murder of her second husband, Henry Stuart. Her uncaring attitude and shunning of the traditional mourning made her look guilty.

in Scotland in her absence. Mary also had her own claim to the English throne through Margaret Tudor, Henry VIII's sister and her grandmother. To Catholic opinion, Mary had a stronger claim to the English throne than Elizabeth. Despite all Elizabeth's best efforts, her reign was not as secure as she would have liked. Luckily, Mary's choice of husbands would soon make her very unpopular.

Darnley: Murderous Intentions

Mary, Queen of Scots, married Henry, Lord Darnley, in 1565. Henry was a Stuart with his own claim to the English throne through his grandmother, Margaret Tudor's marriage to Archibald Douglas, whom she married less than a year after James V's death in 1513. Henry Stuart was a vain, foolish and selfish man, with few scruples.

Above: Mary, Queen of Scots' second husband, the dashing Lord Darnley, is pictured here. An aggressive and arrogant man, Henry expected Mary to submit her authority to him completely and was not above using violence to get his way.

Mary refused to grant Stuart the Crown
Matrimonial—the right to rule equally—which would
have meant the throne would pass to him if Mary died
without issue. Stuart reacted badly to this, as he had
expected his dutiful wife to pas her authority straight to
him. The couple also disagreed on religion, with Mary
a devout Catholic. Despite his bad attitude, narcissism
and a worsening drinking problem, Mary fell pregnant
soon after their marriage. However, rumors came to
light that Stuart was not the father of Mary's unborn
child. The man in question was believed to be David
Rizzio, Mary's Italian secretary with whom she was

**Above: The murder of David Rizzio is depicted in this striking image.
Rizzio is shown being viciously and repeatedly stabbed in what is
clearly the Queen's bedchamber. Darnley was integral to the plot
although he did not bloody his own hands by stabbing Rizzio himself.**

thought to have had an affair. Mary thought highly
of Rizzio, but he was Catholic and a foreigner who
had gained a prized position in Mary's court, so he
quickly became unpopular. Many were jealous of
his relationship with the Queen and this was used to
inspire Protestant rebels to turn against him. Henry
Stuart is believed to have been deeply involved in the

TUDOR DRESS

FROM ELIZABETH'S EXQUISITE dresses, lavishly designed to outshine every woman near her, to the dashing men of court clad top to toe in finery, Tudor nobles knew how to dress. Henry VIII's famously boxy appearance was due to a short, voluminous coat, which left much of the legs on show, encased in only tight hose. In comparison, the women favored a more structured silhouette. Stiff corsets were worn—sometimes made from steel—which gave woman a triangular shape, contrasted by a full skirt.

Commoners would wear much more practical clothing in muted colors, as the luxurious silks and velvets in rich shades were far more expensive to buy. Clothing would also be made from cheaper, warmer materials such as wool. Portraits of Elizabeth (and many nobleman of the period) show her wearing a ruff, the pleated fabric ruffle at her neck. Ruffs could be up to a foot wide and had a practical use, in that they could be changed easily, allowing the wearer to remain in the rest of their clothing for longer!

plot, even hoping that Mary would miscarry her baby through the shock of Rizzio's murder.

Bursting into Mary's private chambers, where the Queen—then seven months pregnant—was entertaining Rizzio, the rebels demanded that he was handed over to them. Rizzio reputedly shielded himself behind his pregnant lover's body, begging for his life. Mary refused at first, but was herself held at gunpoint. Rizzio was viciously stabbed over 50 times until his pleas were silenced. His body was then thrown down the stairs, stripped of all valuables and finally tossed into a grave in Holyrood cemetery, Edinburgh.

> The actual reason behind Rizzio's death is cause for speculation. Darnley was jealous and tempestuous, certainly capable of wanting his wife's lover dead.

Mysterious Death

The actual reason behind Rizzio's death is cause for speculation. Darnley was jealous and tempestuous, certainly capable of wanting his wife's lover dead. Elizabeth herself is rumored to have supported plans to destabilize the Scottish Queen, although whether she would have knowingly gone as far as having a heavily pregnant woman held at gunpoint is unlikely. But Mary proved herself of stern stuff. She lived through the terrifying attack and carried her unborn child safely to term. Unfortunately for the Scottish Queen, life still had a lot more to test her with.

Darnley himself, always unpopular, was now practically an outcast. While relations between him and Mary improved on the birth of their son, James,

Below: Mary's second marriage was even briefer than her first. Darnley met a sticky end in February 1567, after being wed for less than two years. Note the bodies of Darnley and his groom at the top right of the image, both men having fled the house during the night.

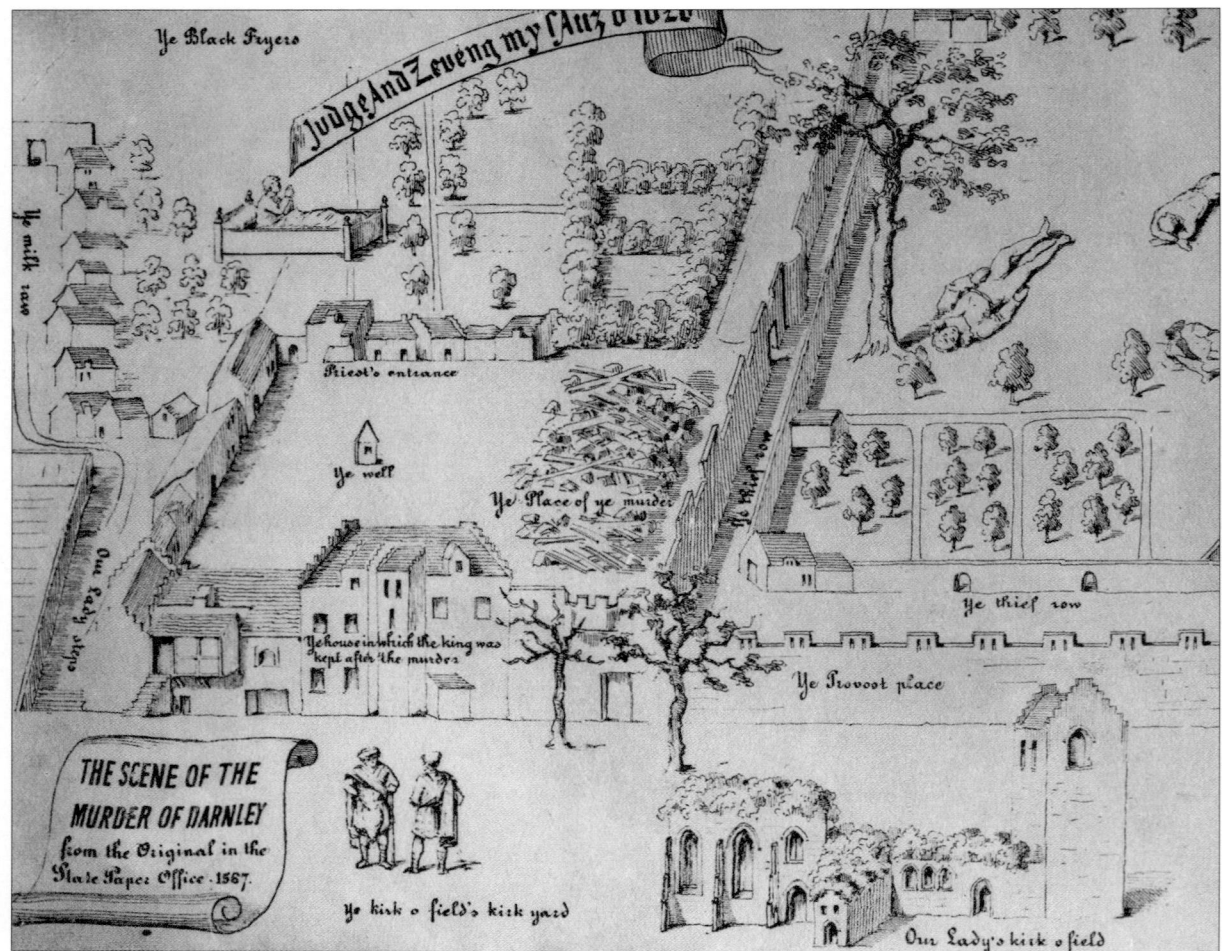

Stuart still demanded that Mary bestow the Crown Matrimonial rights upon him, hoping to snatch the absolute power of the King. But the controversy of Mary and her men was not over yet. On February 10, 1567, Darnley was in Kirk o' Field, one of Mary's estates near Edinburgh. Nothing was out of the ordinary until the early hours of the morning, when two barrels of gunpowder placed directly under the foundations of Darnley's sleeping quarters exploded. Adding to the intrigue, when Darnley and his valet's bodies were found, they had not died in the blast. They lay in the grounds, with Darnley still in his night attire, and near the bodies lay a cloak, coat, dagger and chair. Closer examination found something stranger still— they had both been strangled.

> ... when Darnley and his valet's bodies were found, they had not died in the blast ... they had both been strangled.

Hepburn: Delusions of Power

Already steeped in suspicion after Stuart's death, Mary did herself no favors with her second marriage. She had made it known that she wanted rid of her unsatisfactory husband, and the careless Queen found herself surrounded by more intrigue when she married James Hepburn, Earl of Bothwell, on May 15, 1567,

BOTHWELL'S WOMEN

JAMES HEPBURN (pictured) had quite a past long before his dastardly conduct with Queen Mary. He was still married to his second wife, Jean Gordon when he carried off the Queen. Hepburn then divorced Jean on May 7—on the grounds of his adultery with one of her servants— just eight days before he married Mary. Making his behavior even more dubious was the fact that Hepburn was already married under Norwegian law. He had wed Anna Throndsen in 1559, whom he brought home to Scotland from Norway.

When he ran out of money Hepburn sent his bride back to Norway to ask for more money from her wealthy family. She never returned to him. On his arrival at Bergen in Norway, Anna and her family discovered his return and had him arrested for abandonment. When the news of his suspected involvement in Darnley's murder broke, King Frederick imprisoned Hepburn in Dragsholm Castle. Hepburn is thought to have spent the final years of his life chained to a pillar, growing progressively insane until his death in 1578. His ghost is said to haunt the castle grounds to this day!

just three months after Darnley's murder. Hepburn was one of the men accused of murdering Darnley—he stood trial but was fully acquitted.

Controversy remains over the conditions of this marriage. Mary was making her way to Edinburgh from Stirling, where she had been visiting her son, James, for what would be the last time. On April 24, during the journey, Mary was abducted by Hepburn and his men. She was told that they had come to protect her from plots on her life. Hepburn took Mary to his castle in Dunbar, where it is alleged that he raped her to ensure she would comply. This story remains controversial as it is unclear how far Mary was a willing participant in the abduction, as she was previously thought to have been fond of Hepburn. He and Mary were married eight days later on May 15, 1567. Whatever the circumstances of their union, the marriage remained highly contentious and split the Lords and country down the middle. Violence erupted in June, at which stage Hepburn fled the country, never to see Mary again. He ended up in Norway, where his past caught up with him and he spent his last days in prison until his death.

> Hepburn ... and Mary were married eight days later ... Whatever the circumstances of their union, the marriage remained highly contentious and split the Lords and country ...

Mary's Mistakes

Hepburn's actions resulted in Mary fleeing to England to escape the wrath of her countrymen, all remaining support for the Queen washed away by her feckless behaviour. She was imprisoned in Loch Leven castle, on the isolated island in the middle of the Loch. Things went from bad to worse when she suffered a miscarriage, only then discovering that she had been

Left: Mary, Queen of Scots was forced to abdicate in July 1567, when her rash decisions became too erratic for even her supporters to explain away. Even in this tense painting, Mary looks defiantly at her accusers before signing her kingdom over to her son, James.

Mary spent the following year under virtual house arrest as she was moved from various locations … while Elizabeth took her time in deciding the Scottish Queen's fate.

carrying twins. Shortly after, Mary was compelled to abdicate, passing the throne to her son James, then only one year old.

In May 1568, Mary escaped her prison. She still had some supporters who wanted to reinstate her as Queen, but her forces were defeated at Langside by James Stewart—Mary's half-brother and Regent of Scotland—and Mary fled to England for safety. It was here that she made yet another mistake. Believing that she could trust her cousin Elizabeth, she requested

Above: The castle of Loch Leven looks peaceful and idyllic here, but its isolated position surrounded by water made it the ideal location for a prison. Mary was only able to escape because she was aided by the brother of the castle's owner, Sir William Douglas.

help in reclaiming the Scottish throne. Mary spent the following year under virtual house arrest as she was moved from various locations, never too close to Scotland or London, while Elizabeth took her time in deciding the Scottish Queen's fate. An inquiry was held, during which letters between Mary and Hepburn came to light, although their validity is unproved. The eventual result of the inquiry was inconclusive. James Stewart remained Regent of Scotland with a Protestant government in power and Mary languished in English custody. With no charges proven, she was treated well but her movements were much curtailed and the crafty Queen was closely watched.

In 1571, Francis Walsingham, Elizabeth's spymaster, uncovered a plot to assassinate the Queen and replace

Above: Mary looks favorably at her rescuers as they spirit her away from captivity. The image was painted by William Craig Shirreff in 1805. By this time, most of Mary's indiscretions had been forgotten and she was remembered as the romantic heroine she is seen as here.

THE CASKET LETTERS

CONVENIENTLY FOR ELIZABETH, the discovery of a silver casket containing letters between Mary and Hepburn was discovered in 1567. Moray presented these letters as proof that Mary was embroiled in the plot to kill Darnley, as they apparently stated in her own hand that she hoped Hepburn would soon rid her of him. At the time, the letters were largely regarded as genuine, however Mary insisted that they were forgeries and later historians have speculated on the possibility of forged text being inserted into Mary's genuine letters. The originals were thought to have been burned in 1584 by James VI, Mary's son and then King of Scotland, so the truth may never be uncovered.

Right: The "secret correspondence" between Mary, Queen of Scots, and her accomplices was often written in cipher, or code. This example shows the different symbols and letters used to make up the cipher, which Babington here reveals to Walsingham's agents.

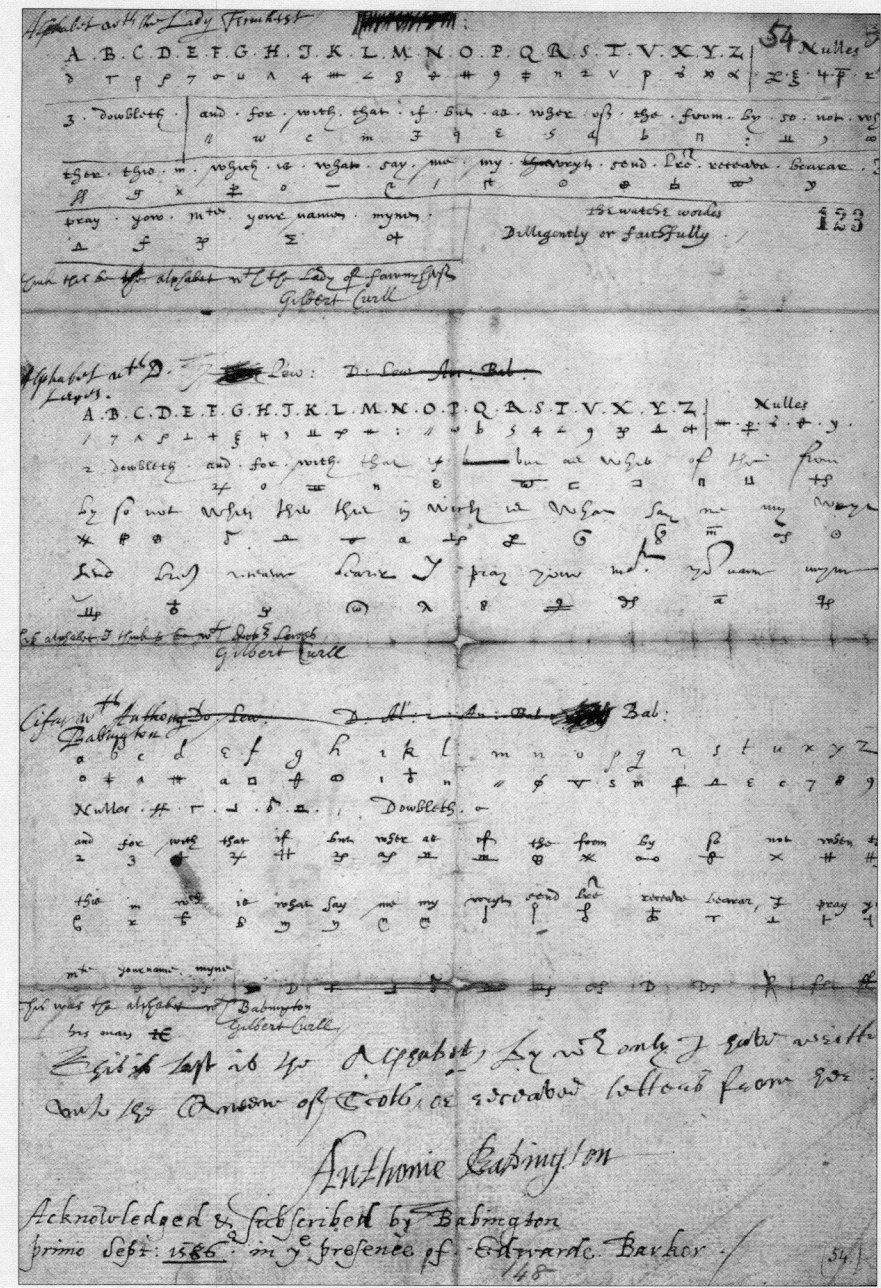

... the forth Duke of Norfolk ... had wanted to marry Mary, but Elizabeth refused the union and threw him in the Tower ...

her with Mary. The Queen of Scots had become something of an icon for Catholic dissidents to gather around. Thomas Howard was the forth Duke of Norfolk and Elizabeth's great-uncle. He had wanted to marry Mary, but Elizabeth refused the union and threw him in the Tower in 1569 to cool his passion. In retaliation, Howard joined forces with Roberto di Ridolfi, a banker from Florence who raised foreign troops to depose Elizabeth and restore England to Catholicism under Mary and Howard. Both were in agreement, largely due to Elizabeth's treatment of them and their own personal lust for power. The Ridolfi plot grew in support and could have been a real threat to Elizabeth, had her intelligence network not informed her of it. Ridolfi's messenger was arrested on arrival at Dover, and the whole plot was revealed under torture. Howard was sent to the Tower and executed in 1572. Ridolfi only escaped punishment by never returning to England.

However, Elizabeth could not yet rest easy. As long as Mary lived she could be used as a figurehead for any Catholic uprising that gathered enough

Above: Elizabeth finally signed the death warrant for Mary, Queen of Scots after she was given irrefutable proof of Mary's involvement in plots to depose her. Elizabeth was later furious when Mary was executed, saying that she had never wanted the warrant acted upon.

MARY THE MARTYR

MARY DRESSED HERSELF carefully for her execution, playing the role of Catholic martyr to the end, despite the hypocrisy of her affairs and collusions. She carried a crucifix in her hand and wore another round her neck. When her black cloak was removed, she was left wearing a dress of deep red, symbolizing the color of religious martyrs.

Mary went to her executioner praying to God and encouraging the crowd to pray with her. After three strokes of the axe her head was severed from her body. Mary had been carrying her small terrier in her gown, which struggled after her death and caused people to believe her headless body was moving!

Conscientia nulle testes

Tyrones   false   Submission   afterwards   rebelling.

Above: Despite Spanish support, O'Neill's uprising ended with Elizabeth's forces crushing the Irish. Here pictured is Hugh O'Neill when he finally submitted to the English in 1603. Elizabeth died before the Irish issue could be fully resolved, until James I ended the fighting.

force. In 1583, with Mary still under house arrest in England, Francis Throckmorton conspired with his father, Nicholas, plus French and Spanish dignitaries to replace Elizabeth with Mary and return England to Catholicism. Walsingham uncovered the plot and arrested Throckmorton, who confessed under torture. Throckmorton was executed in 1584 for high treason. The result of this and the Ridolfi plot was that the Bond of Association was passed that same year, which made it punishable by death to attempt to depose or assassinate Elizabeth I. It also included the stipulation that anyone in the line of succession could be removed from this line and executed even if the plot was carried out in their ignorance. Should she decide to do so, Elizabeth now had the ammunition she needed

> … the Bond of Association … made it punishable by death to attempt to depose or assassinate Elizabeth I.

to execute Mary, leaving her unable to even plead ignorance of these intrigues.

Despite these measures to ensure Elizabeth's safety, yet another plot to replace her with Mary was uncovered in 1586. The Babington Plot saw France and Spain join forces again under Philip II of Spain—whom Elizabeth had refused to marry after her sister's death—to depose the Queen and restore the Catholic faith under Mary. The loyal Walsingham used a double agent to smuggle letters to Mary, realizing that she would need to incriminate herself to prove her involvement and warrant her arrest under the terms of the Bond of Association. The conspiracy worked perfectly and Walsingham soon had his proof, written in Mary's own hand. A total of 16 men were executed for treason before Mary herself was beheaded on 8 February 1587, her cousin Elizabeth having signed her death warrant.

Beyond the Pale

While the various plots of assassination, her intriguing private life and the defeat of the Spanish Armada often take precedence when describing Elizabeth's reign, the harsh treatment of hostilities in Ireland should not be glossed over. With a largely Catholic faith, the Irish had suffered the same religious reforms as England and were heartily tired of religious doctrine being imposed on them by the English monarch. Elizabeth also feared a Spanish attack through the supportive Irish borders. Lands throughout Ireland were therefore granted to English nobles to keep them under control and weaken the nation's chances of banding together. However, a phase of uprisings culminated in Elizabeth employing a scorched earth policy in 1582. Here, lands were burned, destroying crops and all matter of livelihoods. The resulting devastation saw over 30,000 men, women and children die from starvation in Munster alone. Rebellions built up until things reached boiling point in 1594.

With the vicious scorched earth policy realized and the stench of burning still fresh in their nostrils and memories, the Nine Years' War began in 1594 and would rage until Elizabeth's death. While in previous years the chieftains had been too fragmented to band together successfully, two chieftains called Hugh O'Neill and Hugh Roe O'Donnell banded together to fight against the English rule they had long endured. With many resentful of Elizabeth's intentions to advance this rule across the entire country, as well as many Catholics wanting to rid themselves of Protestantism, O'Neill had enough support in Ireland to make England fear for the safety of her borders. In addition, O'Neill sought help from Scottish mercenaries and Elizabeth's old adversary, Philip II. This support, along with Scottish aid and Irish mercenaries, boosted his troops to over 8000 men, an unprecedented number with which to attack the English. By 1601, many Irish were starving and it was only the arrival of Spanish support in the same year that kept the war going.

The Nine Years' War caused a strain on Elizabeth's army throughout the rest of her reign, with peace only being settled when James I ended the conflict. This was partly due to the fact that its huge expense was crippling to England. Peace was preferable, but it was also a lot cheaper.

After years of negotiations and squabbling, the Battle at Yellow Ford saw a victory for Ireland when 2000 English troops were killed. This led to further uprisings across the country. In response, Elizabeth sent Robert Devereux—Dudley's stepson and Elizabeth's new pet at court—to Ireland in 1599 with 17,000 Englishmen prepared to quell the Irish uprisings. However, his occupation was short-lived and unsuccessful. The troops were spread too thin and many were ambushed, with thousands of others dying from disease brought on by unsanitary living conditions. Devereux agreed a truce with O'Neill and returned to England in 1599, defying Elizabeth's orders for him to remain. On presenting himself to the Queen, who was much displeased at his return, Devereux found himself charged with desertion of duty. Cecil and Raleigh were united in trying to get rid of him, but such was his influence and popularity with Elizabeth that she let him off gently.

… lands were burned … The resulting devastation saw over 30,000 men, women and children die from starvation in Munster …

Devereux later signed his own death warrant when he and his men tried to force his way into the Queen's chambers in 1601. He was then arrested, tried and found guilty of treason, having the dubious claim to fame of being the last person ever beheaded on Tower Green.

Back in Ireland, George Carew—Devereux's replacement—managed to crush the worst of the rebellion by 1601. The crippling cost and damage did not entirely fade from memory until Elizabeth's death. The Queen had proven how brutal and decisive she could be in the face of adversity. These traits would be proven once again during the Spanish Armada and its aftermath.

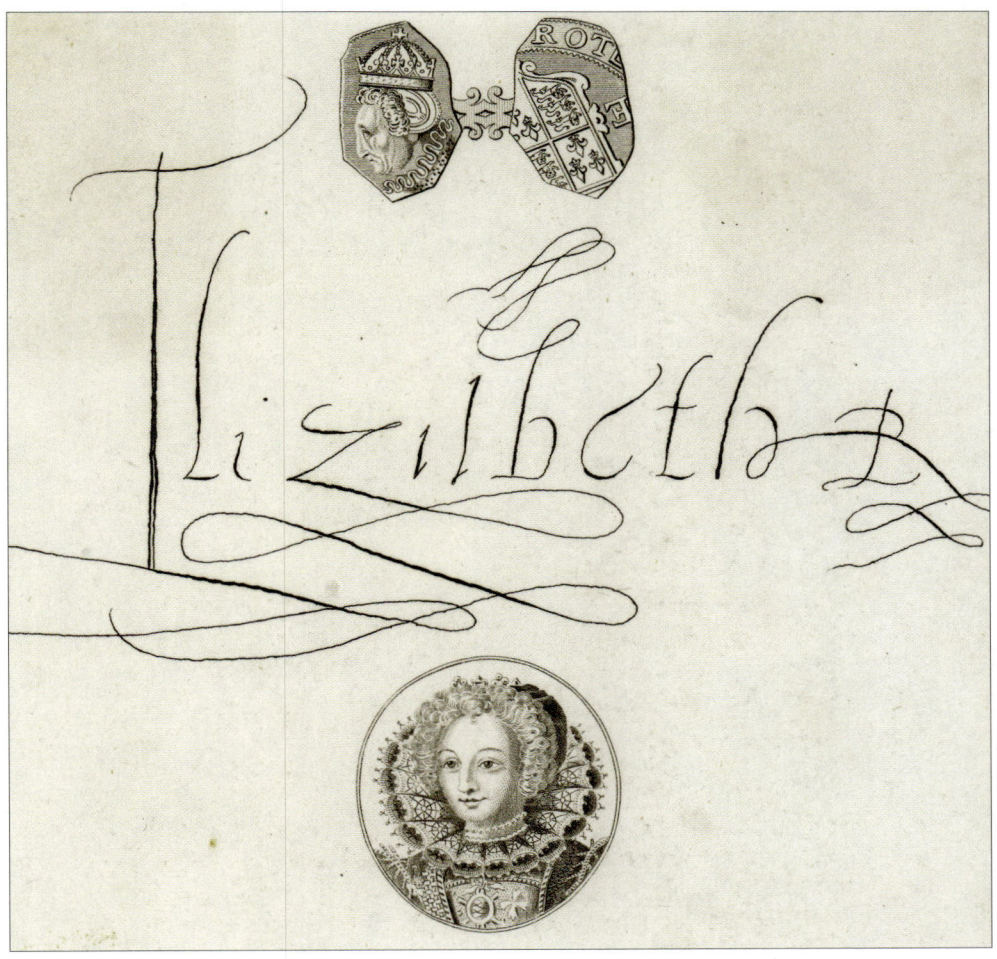

Opposite: In this famous and memorable image, Elizabeth is dressed from head to toe in a deep red, the color mirrored throughout the rest of the image. Purposefully depicting the Queen as strong and in control, Elizabeth's haughty expression dares anyone to defy her authority.

Right: This is Elizabeth's signature, hinting at a woman of bold and determined character. Fittingly, this signature sealed the death warrant for Robert Devereux, the Queen's one-time favorite. He became yet another man that Elizabeth cast aside rather than submit to.

Her vanity, jealousy, fierce nature, religious indifference and a nature so mercurial that it drove members of her council to distraction …

A True Queen

Shadows of her father can be seen in Elizabeth's one-sided and self-serving views, but still it is Mary who is "Bloody" and vicious, perhaps as she attacked people's faith and beliefs. Elizabeth, however, was by no means seen as perfect or flawless. Her vanity, jealousy, fierce nature, religious indifference and a nature so mercurial that it drove members of her council to distraction and rage could have made her despised and ridiculed across Europe. But her immense charisma, glory, love of her people and ability to turn a phrase made her beloved and almost worshipped by many. The cult of the Virgin Queen became part of English culture from the time of her reign, which is unusual. It is generally years after someone's death that his or her own persona becomes moulded into a beloved icon (as with Henry VI, the miracle worker) or a force for evil (as with Bloody Mary). It is a sign of Elizabeth's own strength of character and ability to present herself in the right way that she became the stuff of legend even before her death. Her power reaches from beyond the grave and continues to enthrall to this day.

The Chancellors Seat.

VII

ELIZABETH I:
THE TUDOR LEGACY

Having rid herself of potential usurpers, crushed troublesome neighbors and led her council a merry dance of procrastination for over two decades, Elizabeth would now spread her rule across the seas. The Spanish may be coming, but Gloriana intended to send them packing. While her gaze was on the English borders, the attention of her beloved subjects was firmly on the Queen. England was about to usher in a golden age of arts, theatre and literature in which she was given a starring role.

"I may not be a lion, but I am lion's cub and I have a lion's heart."

Spain had long been taking advantage of trade routes and settlements to grow wealthy from exploring and foreign business. Having acquired lands in the Americas in the fifteenth century, Spain began the colonization of the New World. Christopher Columbus had brought the gift of Christianity, but took slaves, vast riches and many lives in return.

Opposite: This sumptuous painting shows Elizabeth I opening her Parliament with just as much authority as any of the great Kings that preceded her. Despite plots, religious disputes and rebellions, Good Queen Bess held the love of her council and country alike.

Francis Drake came from a farming family, but took to sea when the family moved to Kent from Devon due to the religious uprisings under Edward VI. He proved a natural sailor whose run-ins with the Spanish inspired a vengeful attitude he would later be renowned for. Drake first set sail with the authority of Elizabeth in 1572, aiming to capture a town in Panama as an English stronghold. While this was unsuccessful, he and his crew made a great fortune in plunder and Drake returned to England a wealthy man.

Elizabeth was delighted with her swashbuckling adventurer and, eager to take advantage of lucrative trade routes long utilized by Spain, the Queen financed an expedition for Drake to explore what lay beyond the New World and make a full circumnavigation of the globe in 1577. Elizabeth made it clear that any damage he could cause to the Spanish while on this mission would be looked upon favorably, an addendum Drake took great pleasure in.

Five ships left England in December, but due to bad weather they became separated, so the *Golden Hind* (originally the *Pelican*) completed the circumnavigation alone. The expedition took almost three years. Drake returned on September 26, 1580,

Below: This impressive map by Nicola van Sype, dated 1581, depicts Drake's circumnavigation of the globe (show with the pale dotted line), which began in 1577. Drake won the hearts of the English public, even if the Spanish were not so enamored of his antics.

> Elizabeth made it clear that any damage he could cause to the Spanish ... would be looked upon favorably ...

to be met at the dock by an adoring Queen who immediately bestowed a knighthood upon him. Already deemed a success by its achievement, the expedition was thought to be a miracle of God when Drake shared the treasure won from *Nuestra Senora*

de la Conception, a Spanish galleon the *Golden Hind* had captured and looted. With six tons of gold, Elizabeth earned enough to pay off her entire foreign debt. Drake would go on to defend his country in the Spanish Armada, aiding the English victory.

In 1585, Elizabeth again called upon her trusty pirate. Drake was to lead 25 ships into Spanish waters and cause as much damage as he could to Spanish acquisitions in the New World. This Drake performed admirably. He was able to take several cities in the West Indies, including San Domingo, the prosperous capital of the Spanish New World. Several cities were plundered, wrecked and ransomed by Drake's pirates,

Above: Elizabeth I knights Francis Drake aboard the *Golden Hind* in 1580 on the completion of his circumnavigation. An excellent example of propaganda painting, Elizabeth is the powerful monarch whose subjects will travel the length and breadth of the world for her.

causing huge damage to Spanish credit and trade, and making the name of Drake notorious.

Drake struck again in 1587, when he laid siege to Cadiz in southwest Spain. This time Drake was to cause damage to the Spanish fleet, which Philip II was readying to set against England. In April 1587, Drake's fleet—under his lead on the *Elizabeth Bonaventure*—roared through the Spanish, pushing back the galleons

BOWLS BEFORE BATTLE

WHEN THE FIRST of the Spanish fleet were sighted at Plymouth, sending the English into a frenzied rush of preparation, it is rumored that Drake did not spring into action to defend his beloved country. Instead, the dashing brigand calmly finished the game of bowls he was enjoying (as depicted below), before making his way to take on the might of the Armada. Drake's knowledge of the local tides meant he had no need to rush.

Drake's cavalier attitude belies his anti-Catholic stance and hatred of the Spanish, by whom many of his shipmates suffered in his early days of seafaring.

that had been sent out to intercept them and destroying or capturing several ships. Many costly provisions that the Spanish had worked for months to build up were lost within hours.

Leaving Cadiz and heading for Portugal, Drake's fleet attacked and destroyed every Spanish ship they encountered, allowing nothing to get past their mighty convoy. As a consequence, the Spanish now knew Drake as *El Draque* (the dragon) and Philip II personally set a high price on Drake's head. However, the pirate's luck held as Drake was able to capture the *São Filipe,* a Portuguese ship returning from the West Indies. This capture saw Drake amass another fortune in gold, silks and spices. A total of 100 Spanish vessels were put out of action and the planned Spanish invasion was set back by an entire year.

Opposite: The waters of this painting seethe with danger and tension, mirroring how the Spanish fleet at Cadiz must have felt on facing the raid in April 1587, which delayed the Armada by almost a year.

Curtailing the Catholics

Even with Drake making sport with the Spanish fleet on her express command, Elizabeth took precautions to assure the safety of the English. Robert Dudley was sent to the Netherlands in 1585 as a result of the Treaty of Nonsuch, the signing of which Philip II took as a declaration of war. The treaty had come about after Alessandro Farnese, the Duke of Parma and Philip's Governor General in the Netherlands, laid siege to Antwerp in 1585, forcing Protestants out of the city and placing a large portion of the Netherlands under the control of Catholic Spain. Elizabeth reluctantly agreed to supply the Netherlands with enough troops to end the siege, as well as much needed money to support their forces, needing to put a halt to Philip II's expanding dynasty.

The eager, if inefficient, Dudley's role was to do just that, giving just enough support and money to the Dutch as was needed to secure any threat against

> Dudley found it hard to walk a fine line between Elizabeth's exacting expectations and the desires of the oppressed Dutch …

England. But Dudley found it hard to walk a fine line between Elizabeth's exacting expectations and the desires of the oppressed Dutch for Dudley's forces to take up arms with them against the Spanish invaders. He failed and was publically reprimanded by a letter from Elizabeth, who had been furious when Dudley

Below: Determined to defend England against Philip II, Elizabeth earned the anger of Rome by refusing to submit to Catholicism. Here Pope Pius V issues a bull to excommunicate Elizabeth. Like her father, even the anger of God's representative did not dissuade her.

The Popes bull against the Queene.

Above: Spanish ships churn up the sea as they face the might of the British Navy during the Armada. Philip's so-called "invincible fleet" was no match for Drake's sea dogs, who—aided by luck and bad weather—broke up the Spanish fleet in 1588.

Elizabeth knew full well that Philip II had supported the various plots to overthrow her in favor of a Catholic alternative.

accepted the Governor-General title that she refused. She was not blind to her favorite's faults and knew his ambition often caused Dudley to act rashly. Elizabeth was also hesitant to provide too much open support as England was in continued peace talks with Spain (despite Drake's actions, which Elizabeth could always disavow). But any possibility of peace would soon come to nothing.

Spanish Armada

With disputes against Spain a recurring feature of the Tudor reign, it was only under Elizabeth that the uneasy alliance shattered, resulting in out and out war. Elizabeth knew full well that Philip II had supported the various plots to overthrow her in favor of a Catholic alternative. Elizabeth's support of the Protestant Dutch Revolt—half-hearted though it was—had angered Spain further amid fears of Protestantism spreading across Europe. Trade with Spain had been curtailed because of the Revolt and there had been attacks on trade routes and new settlements in the New World, which the cunning Queen was eager to exploit for England, thus further weakening Spanish global influence.

As Elizabeth had been excommunicated for heresy in 1570 by Pope Pius V, the current Pope, Sixtus V, fully supported Philip II in the invasion to force England back to Catholicism, even pledging money (although

---

Sixtus V fully supported Philip II in the invasion to force England back to Catholicism.

---

the devious Pope stipulated that the money would only be given when the fleet actually landed on English shores). One of the final straws was Drake, who raided Cadiz in 1587, destroying a fleet of Spanish ships that were being made ready for the invasion. This, alongside the Treaty of Nonsuch and revenge for Elizabeth's continued flouting of his authority, was cause enough for Philip. It was time to take the "invincible fleet" of the Armada to England.

Spain Prepares for War

Led by the Duke of Medina Sidonia, the Spanish planned to invade England in 1588. Medina was a great general, but very inexperienced in sea battle, having replaced the previous commander just a few months earlier. The entire fleet began to sail from Lisbon in Portugal on May 28, consisting of 130 ships and around 18,000 soldiers, taking a full two days to leave the port. This fleet was joined by an additional 30,000 men from the Spanish Netherlands, meaning that a massive force was heading for the ports of England. The spectacle must have been overwhelming. Negotiations between Spain and England were initially entered into throughout June, but these were abandoned for good by July 16, by which time the English fleet was assembled at Plymouth. Tensions were rising sharply; with 200 ships, the English outnumbered the invaders, yet the Spanish had more available firepower with which to attack.

The English were led by Lord Howard of Effingham, with Vice Admiral Francis Drake supporting. Drake soon assumed effective command

due to his battle experience, which far outweighed Medina Sidonia's, who followed Philip's instructions to the letter even when nature fought against them. Nature had a large part to play in the end, causing the arrival of the Spanish fleet to be delayed in reaching Plymouth, with a few of the ships not even making this first leg of the journey. Sailing on towards the Isle of Wight, the Spanish were followed by English ships on July 19. Although less well armed, the English used their advantage of speed and maneuvrability to avoid close contact fighting, but lost ground when Drake turned back to loot some abandoned Spanish ships under cover of darkness on July 21–22.

The Spanish headed for Calais, meaning to join forces with Parma's army in the Channel. They found it much harder to send and receive communications than planned, so there the fleet waited, eager for word and backup. Taking advantage of the lack of action, Drake pushed the English advantage. He ordered eight of the English warships to be sacrificed as fireships. The mighty vessels were filled with combustibles and set alight before being cast among the Spanish fleet. Under the sight of the fireships bearing down on them the Armada scattered, thereby losing much of their protection. With that, the English fleet moved in for the kill. Getting just close enough to do damage,

---

He ordered eight of the English warships to be sacrificed as fireships … filled with combustibles and set alight before being cast among the Spanish fleet.

Drake and his sea-warriors used the remains of their gunpowder to devastating effect, damaging many Spanish ships without letting them get close enough for boarding, a trick the Spanish had long preferred. When the English began to run out of momentum they pulled back, having blasted a significant hole in the mighty Armada.

Opposite: Elizabeth I is depicted as the Warrior Queen. Painted to capture her at Tilbury, Elizabeth sits atop a white steed, flanked by Dudley and Devereux, as she rouses her troops to victory.

THE PRIVATEERS

A PIRATE BY any other name, a privateer was able to attack foreign ships during times of war with the sanction of their government. Using privateers enabled the crown to benefit from private ships and voyages doing their work for them, without the cost of ships or officers. For the privateers, vast riches could be theirs for the taking, as any booty was split between the crew.

Drake may be the most well known of Britain's privateers, but many braved the seas in search of adventure and fortune, enjoying their work and the spoils it could win them.

> Truth be told, the speech was almost unnecessary as the Spanish were ready to head for home, hungry and battered …

Elizabeth's Victory and the Spanish Defeat

After some respite, with much of the Spanish fleet exhausted and ready to head for home, Elizabeth made the journey to Tilbury to rally her loyal men for the final skirmish. It was here that she made her most famous speech and assured her place in the hearts of her faithful subjects. Truth be told, the speech was almost unnecessary as the Spanish were ready to head for home, hungry and battered, to be tested further by bad luck and bad weather. However, Elizabeth's commanding, majestic words show just how compelling and magnificent she could be, her words eloquently expressing the Queen's passion and courage. Her speech still resonates today and must have been spectacular on the eve of battle, delivered by their Queen and self-styled mother clad in full armor as she rode among her steadfast troops:

We have been persuaded by some that are careful of our safety, to take heed how we commit our selves to armed multitudes, for fear of treachery; but I assure you I do not desire to live to distrust my faithful and loving people. Let tyrants fear. I have always so behaved myself that, under God, I have placed my chiefest strength and safeguard in the loyal hearts and good-will of my subjects; and therefore I am come amongst you, as you see, at this time, not for my recreation and disport, but being resolved, in the midst and heat of the battle, to live and die amongst you all; to lay down for my God, and for my kingdom, and my people, my honor and my blood, even in the dust.

I know I have the body but of a weak and feeble woman; but I have the heart and stomach of a king, and of a king of England too, and think foul scorn that Parma or Spain, or any prince of Europe, should dare to invade the borders of my realm: to which rather than any dishonor shall grow by me, I myself will take up arms, I myself will be your general, judge, and rewarder of every one of your virtues in the field.

I know already, for your forwardness you have deserved rewards and crowns; and we do assure you in the word of a prince, they shall be duly paid you. In the mean time, my lieutenant general shall be in my stead, than whom never prince commanded a more noble or worthy subject; not doubting but by your obedience to my general, by your concord in the camp, and your valour in the field, we shall shortly have a famous victory over those enemies of my God, of my kingdom, and of my people.

> " … for your forwardness you have deserved rewards and crowns; and we do assure you in the word of a prince, they shall be duly paid you …"

Shortly after Elizabeth's iconic speech, the ravaged Spanish fleet headed for home. They sailed around the open seas of Scotland and Ireland, not wanting to face the English in the close quarters of the Channel. However, by a strange coincidence or, as many later

Opposite: In another example of the carefully controlled portraits of Elizabeth, this iconic scene captures the moment that the chivalric Walter Raleigh throws down his new cloak in the path of his Queen, protecting her feet from a muddy puddle that bars her way.

believed, the will of God, the remaining fleet was wrecked by gales and storms, eventually losing more men and ships to the weather than to battle. Only half the "invincible fleet" that left Spain managed the journey home, with many more dying of disease once they had reached the shores of Spain.

In comparison, English losses were relatively minimal (although the English also suffered rampant disease), but there was no out and out victory won by Drake's fleet. However, the fleet had proved its superiority and mastery against a dangerous adversary, which it had defeated and sent away in tatters. National pride was overwhelming and Elizabeth assured her supreme position in both history and the hearts of her people. The belief that God was on her side saw an upsurge in Protestantism, despite such superstitions being a relic of Catholicism. With Elizabeth riding high on her glorious victory, the timing was perfect for further naval expansion and a Counter Armada to be sent against Spain. Although this Counter was largely unsuccessful, the pride of the nation was not to be dented.

> With Elizabeth riding high on her glorious victory, the timing was perfect for … a Counter Armada to be sent against Spain.

While England under Elizabeth had successfully beaten back the Spanish Invasion, there was to be no peace between the enemy countries. Elizabeth was always reluctant to wage unnecessary war. Unlike her father, who sought glory on the battlefield, Elizabeth tried to avoid embroiling her country in a fruitless and expensive conflict, perhaps learning from Mary I's mistake over Calais. However, she was prepared to secure England by any means possible, taking a ruthless and destructive line if events called for it.

Raleigh: The Noble Knight

Walter Raleigh (also spelt Ralegh) came to Elizabeth's attention during his military service in Ireland. He soon became another favorite of the Queen's and is famous for allegedly throwing his cloak across Elizabeth's path so that her feet stayed dry—the epitome of courtly

Above: In another triumph for the Queen, here Walter Raleigh establishes the colony in Virginia in 1584, claimed in Elizabeth's name. Despite Raleigh's hopes, the colony never came to much. Raleigh was later stripped of privileges following his unsanctioned marriage.

chivalry. Raleigh looked to the New World as the future expansion of England and travelled to Roanoke, North Carolina, in 1584 with the intention of setting up a colony in Virginia. While his efforts were unsuccessful, Elizabeth was not put off and kept her new darling close to her, making him Captain of the Guard in 1587, then Governor of Jersey in 1600. Despite Devereux's spiteful remarks—Devereux was openly jealous of Raleigh and tried to sway the Queen against him—Elizabeth awarded Raleigh control over wine licenses and cloth export, making him rich and influential. His star was on the ascendant and Raleigh might even have supplanted the conceited Devereux from the Queen's side had it not been for his marriage.

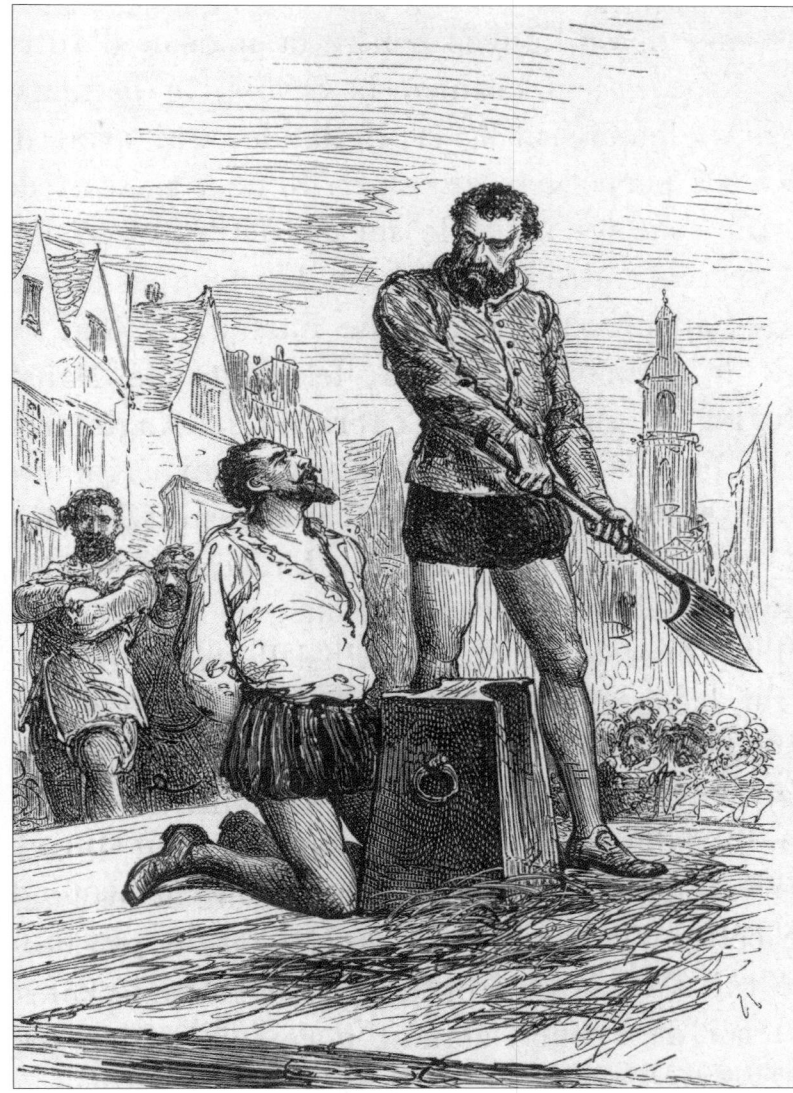

Left: Despite falling out of Elizabeth's favor due to his secret marriage, Raleigh was reconciled to the mercurial Queen towards the end of her life. It was not until his continued warmongering with Spain threatened the uneasy peace James I had secured that Raleigh's luck ran out. He was executed in 1618.

buy freedom with his existing wealth, but no longer held a position at court.

Raleigh turned this expulsion to his favor, using his new freedom to travel to the New World and Guyana. Raleigh hoped to establish settlements and was also seduced by tales of the fabled El Dorado, the legendary city of gold. He never found the city, but remained convinced of its existence and returned to the New World with his son, Walter (also known as Watt) in 1617. This voyage was a disaster and brought about Watt's death. Raleigh himself was later executed by James I for risking a recurrence of the war with Spain after James had brokered peace on Elizabeth's death.

Prior to her death, Raleigh rejoined Elizabeth's court at her side, becoming a member of parliament for Devon, Dorset and Cornwall. His adventures made him a popular public figure, although he was disliked by many nobles and council members. A hero to England, Raleigh remains a romantic gallant, whose actions never quite lived up to his great expectations.

Fall from Grace

Elizabeth was vain to the point of narcissism and expected her favored subjects to only have eyes for her. When Raleigh secretly married his love Elizabeth Throckmorton (who, to compound matters, was a relation of Francis Throckmorton, who had been executed for plotting to depose Elizabeth), Elizabeth was incandescent with rage. She sent both Raleigh and Elizabeth to the Tower, stripping Raleigh of his prominent titles and source of wealth. He was able to

> Raleigh hoped to establish settlements and was also seduced by tales of the fabled El Dorado, the legendary city of gold. He never found the city, but remained convinced of its existence …

had brought religious uniformity to England. While Walsingham's religious views were more Puritan than Elizabeth's, he supported her desire to move slowly, thus avoiding the horrific bloodshed of Mary's reign. A nobleman who first worked as an ambassador, Walsingham's true use to Elizabeth came from his subtle and instinctive intelligence gathering, in which he was unparalleled. It was Walsingham who uncovered the Ridolfi plot in 1570, plus the later Throckmorton and Babington plots to depose Elizabeth. Walsingham would even use his network of agents to entrap Mary, Queen of Scots, providing Elizabeth and her council with irrefutable proof of Mary's conspiracy.

Walsingham: The Spymaster

Elizabeth's principal secretary and spymaster, Francis Walsingham extirpated many plots against his beloved Queen, whom he saw as the rightful monarch and savior of England from a despotic papacy. Similarly to Cecil, we see in Walsingham fear of a Catholic ruler on Elizabeth's throne, whose decades as Queen

The ever-vigilant Walsingham would also use his network—which by now spread across Europe and as far as to North Africa, using nobleman, merchants and even ambassadors' advisors—to uncover information about the Spanish Armada. His men would both inform and manipulate, seeking out and taking

MARLOWE'S DEATH

CHRISTOPHER MARLOWE'S ENTIRE life was led under a veil of mystery—a possible homosexual atheist, he is even rumored to have written several of Shakespeare's plays—and the same can be said of his death. A warrant for Marlowe's arrest was issued on May 18, 1593 and Marlowe handed himself in to the council two days later, where he was told to pay a daily visit to the council until he heard differently. This continued until May 30, when Marlowe was suddenly and viciously stabbed to death in what appeared to be a drunken brawl. He had been drinking with fellow employees of Walsingham's and one of them, Ingram Frizer, had engaged him in a quarrel over the "reckoning," or the bill. Claiming it was self-defence, Frizer was tried but pardoned soon after. Rumors of his death include it being faked to enable him to disappear, as well as it being ordered by Raleigh, Cecil or even Elizabeth herself! Whatever the truth, Marlowe remains legendary for his gorgeously crafted dramas as well as his notorious private life.

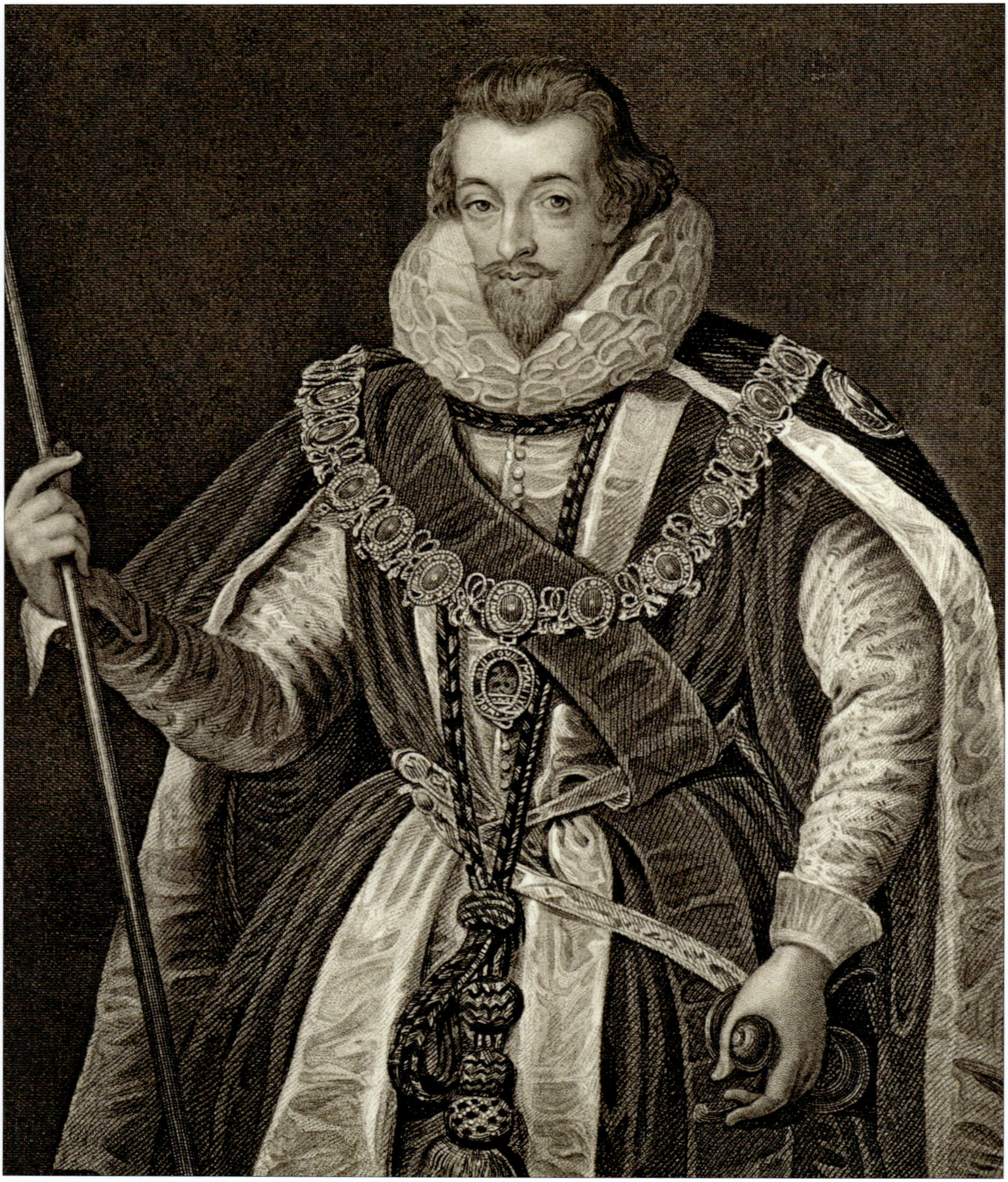

advantage of opportunities to plant misinformation. Walsingham was an ardent supporter of Elizabeth and England, often using his own wealth and resources to uncover information. One of his more famous recruits was the playwright Christopher Marlowe. The nature of the work meant that any spy would keep their profession hidden, but Marlowe is known to have been involved in "matters" for his country. He was also wealthy for a student and was let off a charge for counterfeiting money by Cecil in 1592.

Despite years of ill health, Walsingham continued in his intelligence work up until his death in 1590, ever faithful to his Queen. His daughter, Frances, married three times, her second husband being the petulant

---

> Walsingham clearly saved the life of Elizabeth I several times, but many of his deeds are shrouded in mystery …

---

darling of Elizabeth, Robert Devereux. Walsingham died in debt, possibly due to his outgoings during his time as spymaster, which he was owed by the Crown, and left behind a controversial legacy. Walsingham clearly saved the life of Elizabeth I several times, but many of his deeds are shrouded in mystery and Walsingham was not above using entrapment or force to get his way. However, we know little of a concrete nature on this most elusive of Elizabeth's men.

Robert Cecil: The Fixer

Walsingham's death left the position of secretary of state open, which was filled by a new favorite of Elizabeth's. Robert Cecil was William Cecil, Lord Burghley's son, who had been part of the Privy Council since 1591. His father's death in 1598 saw Robert ascend to a position as Elizabeth's most trusted advisor, like his father before him. The Cecils stand apart as remaining constant supports throughout the Queen's tumultuous reign. Their steady positions within the

Opposite: Robert Cecil, the son of Elizabeth's trusted advisor and friend, William Cecil. Aptly managing the sometimes tricky transition from one monarch to the next, Cecil saw the end of the Tudor monarchy and the beginning of the Stuart era under James I.

Above: Robert Devereux, the Earl of Essex, was a charming and intense character. Believing himself to be indispensible to Elizabeth, he took liberties with the Queen and was often forgiven. He was also insanely jealous and tried to cause Elizabeth to fall out with Raleigh and Cecil.

council perhaps gave them an edge that the more adventurous and dashing courtiers lacked. Robert Cecil could also be relied upon to remain flexible in opinion—a useful tool for any politician within a Tudor court. Robert was not of the striking or handsome stature as most of Elizabeth's favorites, who had a tendency to fill her court with fine-looking flatterers.

Cecil was nicknamed "pygmy" or "elf" by the Queen on account of his hunchback and slight frame. Robert Devereux saw him as a rival for the Queen's affections, and used Cecil's physical deformities against

> Robert Cecil also spent years secretly corresponding with James VI of Scotland, working with him to ensure his accession …

him. However, Robert was an excellent administrator and negotiator who could bide his time far better than Devereux. Cecil would have his revenge on the arrogant Earl when he was tried for treason in 1601.

Robert Cecil also spent years secretly corresponding with James VI of Scotland, working with him to ensure his accession on Elizabeth's death. Sensitive to the Queen's age and her thoughts for a successor, he cleverly ensured his own survival after her death with a place of privilege within the new Stuart council. James I of England made him Earl of Salisbury in 1605 and used his subtlety and patience well as a spymaster.

Devereux: The Hothead

Robert Devereux, Earl of Essex and great-nephew of Anne Boleyn, became the object of Elizabeth's favors in 1587, replacing Dudley—who had married Devereux's mother, Lettice Knollys, after the death of his father— as Master of the Horse that same year. On Dudley's death in 1588 Devereux was also awarded Dudley's duty levied on sweet wines, a huge source of revenue. He became a member of the Privy Council in 1593. Arrogantly believing himself to be special to Elizabeth, Devereux could be charming and affable. His youth and eloquence appealed to the aging Queen and made her feel young and beautiful, just as Dudley had once done. While he was permitted a place of honor at her side and on her council, Devereux was hotheaded

> The Earl was said to be furious at Elizabeth for putting other men in a position of power over him.

and rash, making his ambitions to become a great and masterful warlord implausible, to say the least.

While Devereux did uncover and stop a plot against Elizabeth in 1594—when Rodrigo Lopez (thought to have inspired the Shakespearean character of Shylock), her court physician, colluded with Spain to poison her—Devereux never gained the greatness or popularity he felt he so deserved. The Earl was said to be furious at Elizabeth for putting other men in a position of power over him. After being given several chances, he was sent to Ireland to face Hugh O'Neill during the Nine Years' War. This ended in disaster when his inexperienced handling of the troops wasted many lives. He ignored Elizabeth's orders to attack the Irish rebels, instead discussing a truce with O'Neill. This was followed up by his untimely retreat back to London, where Elizabeth blasted his arrogance for not following her orders.

Devereux had finally gone too far and he was placed under house arrest while Elizabeth vacillated over what to do with the upstart Earl. Unable to take punishment, even from his Queen, Devereux plotted a coup to depose her in early 1601. With 200 of his men he called for public support to join him against the Queen. None was forthcoming. The country could see what it had taken Elizabeth so long to notice and knew that Devereux in power would make a disastrous leader. Enough was enough. Devereux was beheaded on February 25 before he could do any more harm.

Anjou: The Patient Suitor

Elizabeth chose not to follow her sister in making an alliance with another country, although precedent had been set for any King Consort to accept restrictive terms, allowing him the title of King of England for the duration of the marriage only. In fact, the first foreign suitor she turned down was Mary's husband, Philip II, who proposed shortly after Elizabeth's coronation. Following her own words and the advice of her council, Elizabeth soon entered into marriage negotiations with Charles II, the Archduke of Austria. These were drawn

out over nearly ten years until forming an English link with the Hapsburgs became less of an issue.

Still able to have children—just—Elizabeth was then pressed into a suit with Henry, Duke of Anjou, followed by his brother, Francis, who became Duke of Anjou on his brother's accession to the French throne as Henry III. The brothers were the sons of Henry II and Catherine de Medici. Francis, now Duke of Anjou, was 24 when he began his suit towards Elizabeth, then 46 years old. The fact that it was very unlikely that Elizabeth would now bear any children and had no clear successor marked out made this marriage imprudent in the eyes of her advisors, who did not want England to fall under French control. However, Elizabeth did seem to at least be fond of Henry, whom she dubbed her "frog," due to a frog-shaped earring he gave her as a gift.

Despite the age difference, Anjou's lengthy courtship of the Queen saw him get the closest to marrying her than any of her other suitors, excepting Dudley. While it may have began as a way of strengthening the union with France, their courtship soon became one of flirtation and romance. It has interesting parallels with Mary's marriage to Philip, both men being foreign and Catholic. It would mean Elizabeth had to suffer sharing her beloved country as well as making a final matrimonial decision that would

> Despite the age difference, Anjou's lengthy courtship of the Queen saw him get the closest to marrying her than any of her other suitors, excepting Dudley.

likely put paid to many of her courtly flirtations. Last, but by no means least, it was increasingly unlikely that Elizabeth would ever bear children and heirs, rendering the whole point of the union moot.

Anjou was not quite what might be expected for a Queen with such high standards. He was the younger brother of a King. He suffered from smallpox as a child, which left his complexion scarred and his stature was insignificant. However, Anjou quickly delighted the Queen with his sophisticated French bearing and manners. Together, they engaged in a courtly dance of romance and flirtation that would continue on and off for three years.

Anjou remained at the English court for months while the question of marriage was debated back and forth at the council. It might have been Elizabeth's intention to delay matters by choosing a controversial match rather than a solid and respectable Englishman who the council would not hesitate over marrying her to. Yet she genuinely seemed to grow fond of Anjou, keeping love letters he sent her and speaking of him warmly. Anjou returned to court in November 1581 in

Below: Elizabeth's "frog" is shown here to be an attractive, well-dressed young man, just the type the now 46-year old Queen would find desirable. Yet even Anjou failed to win her heart.

> The coquettish Queen saw herself as the unhappy maid torn apart from her would-be suitor by circumstances beyond their control.

a last attempt to secure the marriage. It seemed for a while that he was successful, with Elizabeth publically announcing that she would marry the Duke, even presenting him with a ring to bind the promise.

However, Elizabeth's ardour soon grew cold and she fell back on the political conditions and advice of the council. The council certainly gave her a good excuse as many were still opposed to the match and assured the Queen of the public outcry that would surely follow the union. Now running out of patience and justifiably angry, Anjou did himself no favors by expressing his anger. The coquettish Queen saw herself as the unhappy maid torn apart from her would-be suitor by circumstances beyond their control. He finally left Elizabeth and England in 1582, all hope of the union washed away by the Queen's hesitancy and inconstancy. Ironically, on his departure, Elizabeth wrote a loving poem dedicated to him entitled "On Monsieur's Departure," which expresses her "true" feelings as ones of love pushed aside in the name of duty.

Golden Age

Elizabeth's own poetry is an example of the mass of plays and prose that has come to be associated with the golden age of Elizabethan England. This golden age is a well-known concept. When you consider what the country had gone through under the Tudors and in the preceding centuries, it seems apt that a renaissance

Opposite: The playwright William Shakespeare wrote several plays for Elizabeth, in which the Tudors and their ancestors feature positively and prominently.

THE GLOBE THEATRE

WHILE ELIZABETH COULD command a whole company of players to come to her, commoners and anyone not so blessed had to make do with the Globe theatre (as imagined below by a nineteenth century artist), a modern version of which stands on the banks of the River Thames in London. The theatre was originally built in 1598, but memorably burned down in 1613 during a performance of *Henry VIII*. There now stands a replica based on the original amphitheatre design, which opened in 1997.

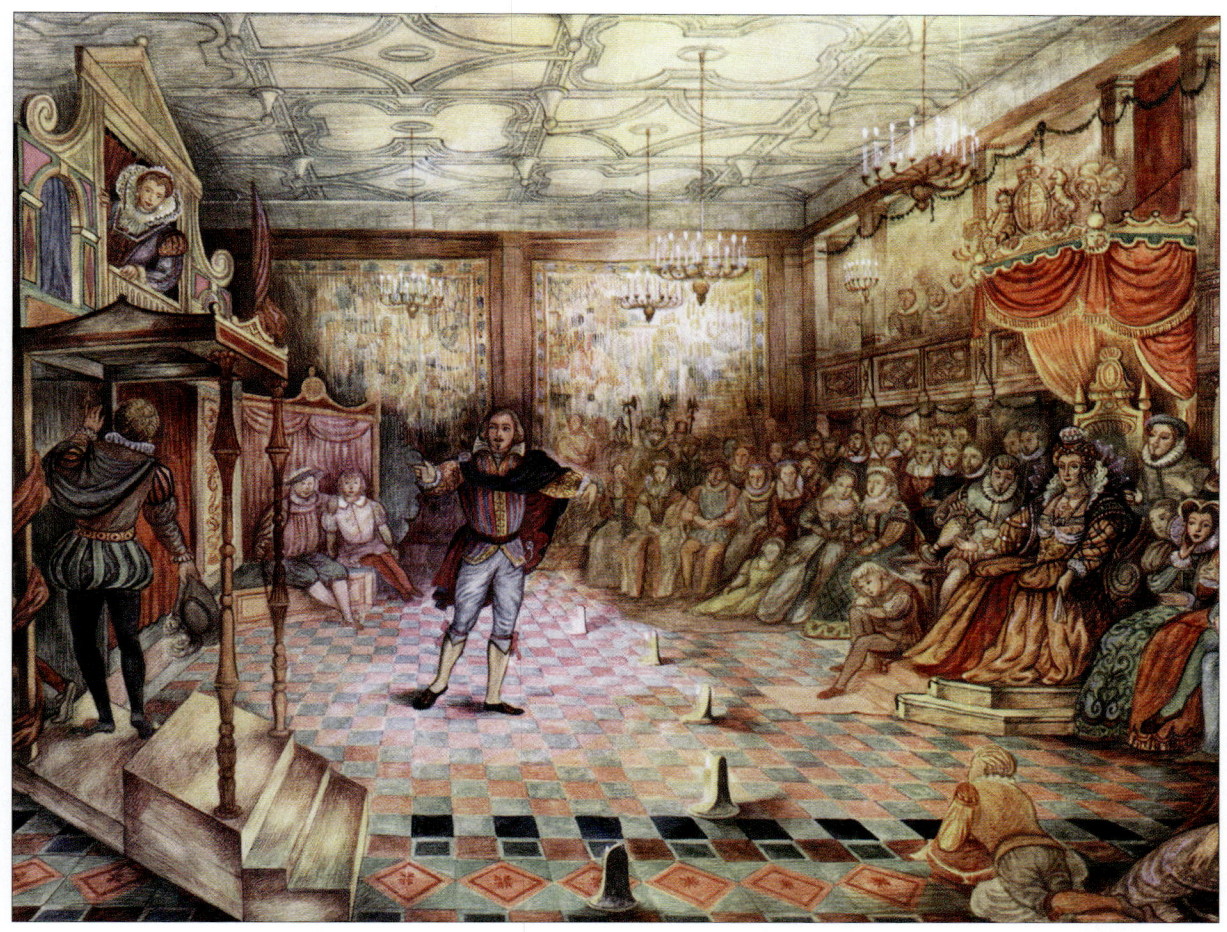

Shakespeare penned plays dedicated to Elizabeth, which were performed for her pleasure in special court performances …

Above: Greenwich Palace was the illustrious backdrop to one of Shakespeare's plays on December 26, 1594, St. Stephen's Day. This illustration shows *Two Gentlemen of Verona* being performed by the Lord Chamberlain's Men for the Queen and her court.

period should come about. Religion was more unified, government more effective and the country had recently won a great victory over the feared and hated Spanish. A flowering of literature, art, drama, music, exploration and discovery occurred, which left behind a legacy of several of England's most famous and well-loved characters.

The most famous of her artistic acolytes is arguably the great William Shakespeare, whose plays and poetry remain adored to this day. Shakespeare penned plays dedicated to Elizabeth, which were performed for her pleasure in special court performances especially for the Queen and her favored subjects. The Lord Chamberlain's men, as the group of players were known, was founded by Henry Carey, who engaged entertainers for Elizabeth's court. Elizabeth is believed to have enjoyed *King Henry IV,* parts 1 and 2, and *Love's Labors Lost.* After expressing her delight at the character of Falstaff, Shakespeare wrote *The Merry*

SPENCER'S EPIC: THE FAERIE QUEENE

EDMUND SPENSER'S EPIC poem, first published in 1590, extols the virtues of the Elizabethan court that the Queen so enjoyed. She herself was famously represented by Gloriana—"great lady of the greatest isle"—the Faerie Queene who symbolizes glory and beauty. We also see the rather more unflattering metaphor of Duessa (or duplicity), who represents Mary, Queen of Scots. The poem can be split into two groups of characters, with virtues largely symbolizing the Protestant church and vices being represented by the Pope, the Roman Catholic Church and its servants. Even Henry VIII appears in the form of a lion, symbolizing honor. Depictions of Elizabeth as Gloriana show her to be forever young and beautiful—just how Elizabeth liked to be remembered!

Wives of Windsor, in which Falstaff, the immensely fat and bigheaded knight, tries to land a rich wife amid a series of comic misfortunes. Shakespeare's beautifully crafted plays cover worlds of magic, mystery and imagination, while his tragedies and histories span the whole range of human emotions, from bliss to despair. One of the most quoted men in history, rumors of Shakespeare's life are notoriously interesting and his life and works remain a source of inspiration and national pride.

> One of the reasons for this large upsurge in creative output during Elizabeth's reign is thought to be a result of the religious reforms away from Catholicism.

One of the reasons for this large upsurge in creative output during Elizabeth's reign is thought to be a result of the religious reforms away from Catholicism. As the rituals of mass became less of a theatrical spectacle and many religious festivals were curtailed, people needed somewhere to go for enjoyment. That place soon became the theatre. While Elizabeth herself was never a confirmed patron of the arts like some of her court, she expected and received their adoration. The Queen was idolized forever by the poet Edmund Spenser, whose *The Faerie Queene* sees her as the goddess-like Gloriana, the adored dream-like woman that Arthur, the chivalric knight, wishes to marry. *The Faerie Queene* has interesting parallels with several members of court, plus other members of the Tudor family, and can be read as an allegory of English life in the sixteenth century, squarely on the side of the Queen and Protestantism.

Elizabeth was an avid lover of music, which she enjoyed playing herself. There was no way she could do without many of the beloved hymns sung during mass that were banned under Edward VI. The Italian composer Gaetano Donizetti was so influenced by the Tudors that he wrote operas based on their lives.

Opposite: The Warrior Queen, Virgin Queen or plain old "Bess" is captured here in this lifelike effigy that adorns her tomb at Westminster Abbey, proof that even Faerie Queens cannot defy time forever.

One of these, *Maria Stuarda*, was in turn based on a play by Freidrich Schiller. It depicts a dramatic fictional meeting between Elizabeth and Mary, who in fact never met. Donizetti was by no means the only musician, artist or writer to be influenced by the lives of the Tudors. The family has inspired many novels, films, plays and television shows, one of the most notorious representations of Elizabeth being "Queenie" in *Blackadder II*. There are even video games in which she makes an appearance!

Legacy

Elizabeth died on March 24, 1603. Finally naming her successor, James VI of Scotland became James I of England—the first monarch to simultaneously rule both countries. Unlike the happiness and relief exhibited at Mary I's death, Elizabeth's loyal subjects were saddened by the loss of their beloved monarch, knowing that their lives would not be the same after her death. She lies in Westminster Abbey near her relations, united in death as they could never be in life. Elizabeth certainly knew how to give her subjects what they wanted. These were by no means prosperous times, but

Above: This allegorical painting shows Henry VIII flanked by his children. Edward is handed the sword of justice. Mary and Philip, left, are with Mars, the God of War, while Elizabeth, right, brings Peace and Plenty to England, marking the end of discord.

the nation was able to share her love for spectacle by means of these pastimes. She had won their hearts a long time ago and showed an astounding ability to hold on to them. Affectionately remembered as Good Queen Bess, Elizabeth's life is an astonishing account of fate, luck, power and personality.

Her place in history was assured even before her death. The mystery with which she led her life still intrigues even if the truth has died with her. Even as her story ends, Good Queen Bess and the entire Tudor family remain constant sources of interest, intrigue and fascination.

Opposite: Instigating the rule of the Stuarts, King James I of England and James VI of Scotland is pictured here, painted by the Flemish artist Paul van Somer. James ruled Scotland, England and Ireland for 22 years, uniting Tudor rose with Scottish thistle.

GLOSSARY

Acts of Succession an act passed by Parliament in 1534 that required all subjects to take an oath recognizing Anne Boleyn as King VIII's legal wife and any children they would have as legitimate heirs to the throne.

annulment a court proceeding that treats a marriage as though it never happened; used by Henry VIII to separate from his wives because divorce was forbidden by the Catholic Church.

Boleyn, Anne the second wife of King Henry VIII and mother of Queen Elizabeth I, she was tried for treason and beheaded in 1536 after she had several miscarriages and did not produce a male heir to the throne.

Catherine of Aragon the first wife of King Henry VIII and mother of Mary Tudor; their marriage was annulled, an event which eventually led to a break between the Catholic church and the monarchy.

Cromwell, Thomas one of King Henry VIII's chief ministers, he was responsible for orchestrating the annulment of the King's marriage to Catherine of Aragon and later contributing to the breakaway of the Church of England from the Catholic Church.

Devise for the Succession a document drafted by the sickly King Edward VI to orchestrate the inheritance of his throne upon his death in reversal of the Third Act of Succession. The document passed over his two sisters in the inheritance and bequeathed it to his cousin, Lady Jane Grey.

Dudley, Robert nobleman and suitor of Elizabeth I for many years, he was a prominent figure in international matters and domestic affairs; one of the chief advocates for the execution of Mary, Queen of Scots.

Edward VI the son of Henry VIII and Jane Seymour, his rule is distinguished for the establishment of Protestantism in England.

Elizabeth I the daughter of Henry VIII and Anne Boleyn and the last monarch in the Tudor dynasty, her reign was distinguished by religious tolerance, the golden age of the British theatre, and exploration. Described as having a mercurial personality, she never married and was beloved by her peoples.

Golden Age term for the renaissance in the theatre and the arts that occurred during the Elizabethan age of England.

Grey, Lady Jane named monarch by her cousin, Henry VI, she ruled England for nine days before being imprisoned in the Tower of London when Mary Tudor took the throne.

Henry VIII the second monarch of the Tudor dynasty, distinguished by his six marriages and his break from the Catholic Church to form Protestantism, or the Church of England.

heresy a religious and civil offence that amounted to treason in the age of the Tudors; Mary I used heresy laws to persecute those who had converted to Protestantism and broken from the Catholic Church.

Mary, Queen of Scots the great niece of Henry VIII, and, according to Catholics, the rightful heir to the throne after Mary I. She was imprisoned in England and eventually executed due to her possible involvement in a conspiracy to take the throne from Elizabeth I.

Mary I the daughter of Henry VIII and Catherine of Aragon, she took the throne from Lady Jane Grey after the death of her half-brother Edward VI. Her reign was distinguished by her persecution of Protestants and her re-establishment of the Roman Catholic Church.

More, Thomas one of Henry VIII's counselors, who opposed the Protestant Reformation; wrote *Utopia*; refused to recognize the annulment of the king's marriage to Catherine of Aragon. He was beheaded because he failed to swear allegiance to the king.

Nine Years War a war between France and a coalition of European powers, including England, the distinguished and strained the last years of Elizabeth I's rule; the conflict ended with James I.

Protestantism a branch of Christianity that originated with the Protestant Reformation; created when Henry VIII decided to remove the Church of England from the Catholic authority of Rome.

Richard III the last King of the House of York, the dynasty that preceded the reign of the Tudors. The Tudor monarchy began when Henry Tudor's army defeated the army of Richard III in a rebellion at the Battle of Bosworth Field.

Third Act of Succession reinstated the right of Henry VIII's daughters, Mary and Elizabeth, to inherit the throne behind their half-brother Edward VI.

FURTHER INFORMATION

Books

Ackroyd, Peter. *Tudors: The History of England from Henry VIII to Elizabeth I*. Oxford: Pan Books, 2013.

Bordo, Susan. *The Creation of Anne Boleyn: A New Look at England's Most Notorious Queen*. New York: Houghton Mifflin Publishing, 2013.

Norton, Elizabeth. *The Temptation of Elizabeth Tudor: Elizabeth I, Thomas Seymour, and the Making of a Virgin Queen*. New York: Pegasus Books, 2016.

Weir, Alison. *The Lost Tudor Princess: The Life of Lady Margaret Douglas*. New York: Ballantine Books, 2015.

Whitelock, Anna. *Mary Tudor: England's First Queen*. New York: Penguin Books, 2016.

Video

Digging for Britain. Directed by James Gray. 2011. United Kingdom: BBC, 2011. DVD.

The Madness of Henry VIII. Directed by Doug Shultz. 2006. New York: National Geographic, 2006. DVD.

INDEX

PICTURE CREDITS